The Political Thought
of Hannah Arendt

The Political Thought of Hannah Arendt

MARGARET CANOVAN

 Harcourt Brace Jovanovich, New York and London

Printed in the United States of America

Library of Congress Cataloging in Publication Data
Canovan, Margaret.
    The political thought of Hannah Arendt.
    Bibliography: p.
    1. Arendt, Hannah.   I. Title.
JC251.A74C28   320.5′092′4   74-3037
ISBN 0-15-172815-1

First published in 1974 by J.M.Dent & Sons Ltd, London
B C D E

Contents

Acknowledgments

Extracts from these works by Hannah Arendt are reprinted by kind permission of the publishers given: *The Origins of Totalitarianism* (Copyright © 1951, 1958, 1966 by Hannah Arendt), Harcourt Brace Jovanovich, Inc., and George Allen and Unwin Ltd; *On Violence* (Copyright © 1969, 1970 by Hannah Arendt), Harcourt Brace Jovanovich, Inc., and Allen Lane The Penguin Press; *On Revolution* (Copyright © 1963, 1965 by Hannah Arendt), The Viking Press, Inc., and Faber and Faber Ltd; *Between Past and Future* (Copyright 1954, © 1956, 1957, 1958, 1960, 1961, 1963, 1967, 1968 by Hannah Arendt), The Viking Press, Inc., and Faber and Faber Ltd; *The Human Condition* (© 1958 by The University of Chicago), The University of Chicago Press.

1

Hannah Arendt's Mode
of Political Thought

'What I propose, . . . is nothing more than to think what we are doing.'[1]

We have often heard it repeated recently that political thought is dead. A place remains, it is said, for works of political science, for the history of ideas, for strictly analytical philosophical consideration of political concepts, and of course for ideological manifestoes; but it is agreed that although the classics of political thought cannot be fitted into any of these categories, there is no future for the kind of activity which they represent. Political thought in the classic sense, which purports to reveal the nature of political things and to provide criteria by which to judge them—political thought in that sense is dead. Ironically enough, during the same years when this obituary was being so plausibly written, it was being challenged by the appearance of a series of striking works of authentic political thinking. Hannah Arendt's work cannot be categorized according to the accepted labels of 'political science', 'conceptual analysis', 'history of ideas' or 'ideological manifesto'; instead, it evidently purports, in the manner of the classics, to arrive at an understanding of politics which will be true to men's experience of political activity, and which will elucidate the place of politics within human life and the criteria appropriate for making judgments about it. These are the claims implicit in her work; and while some might wish to argue that such claims are in principle empty or meaningless, her writings are too able to be dismissed simply on *a priori* grounds.

If the very existence of her work contradicts current assumptions, its content and style present a conscious challenge to academic orthodoxy. In the first place, her work is *political* thought. We have become accustomed of late to seeing the study of politics absorbed peacefully into the ever-expanding realm of sociology. Politics, it seems, is obviously an aspect of Society, the all-encompassing whole; it is therefore appropriate that it should be understood by means of sociological categories. Accordingly the political system is thought of as a sub-system of the social system, political activities are explained in terms of the social functions they fulfil, and political allegiances and opinions are traced to membership of a social class or social role. One of the central purposes of Hannah Arendt's work is to fight against this academic trend, and to redirect our attention away from Society, that self-moving cosmos of which we are presumed to be parts, to Politics: that is, to the public actions and interactions of particular individual men, and the events which they bring about. This change of emphasis is no mere matter of personal preference, for, as we shall see, it represents also an attempt to vindicate human freedom and the significance of individual actions against ways of thought which tend to envisage men as mere cells within the social body. To Hannah Arendt, politics is the realm of freedom, and the defence of politics against sociologism is a defence of human freedom and dignity against determinism and abject submission to fate.

It is equally significant that her work is a series of exercises in political *thought*. She is careful to distinguish *thought* from cognition, the search for specific knowledge, and from logic, the following of rational trains of thought to their logical conclusions [2]—and, again, her emphasis here is polemical, directed against academic orthodoxy, particularly in the social sciences. There is an increasing tendency in academic circles to concentrate upon method, and to assume that the value of conclusions is determined by the validity of the method used. The ideal is a method of approach to a given subject that will be foolproof in the sense that virtually anyone can be taught how to use it and to produce valid knowledge at the end of it. Accordingly information is piled up in universities and sorted out by computers, which can perform the logical operations of the human brain much faster than men. What Hannah Arendt means by thought, however, and what her works present the results of, is a quite different activity. It can be learned and practised, but it cannot be taught by inculcating a method, nor can rules be prescribed for it. It consists in the endless effort of human beings to make sense of what they experience, to get their minds round the things that confront them, the activities they engage in, and above all the events that happen among them. Her work is political thought, not in the sense of being the application of a pre-existing method, whether scientific or philosophical, to political material, but in the sense of representing the free play of an individual mind round politics, making sense of political events and placing them within an unfolding understanding of all that comes within that mind's range. Thinking is the faculty that creates cosmos out of chaos, that gives us, instead of bits of unrelated data or self-enclosed chains of reasoning, a mental world to move in that is adequate to reality. Such thinking is necessarily an individual activity. Men may be able to apply scientific method as a team (though hardly to make the great conceptual leaps which bring about revolutions in science); they may be able to reason in unison, being drawn along irresistibly by the force of logic (a mode of thought that, unchecked by freer modes, seems to Hannah Arendt to have a peculiar affinity with totalitarianism [3]): but they can only think alone, or, in the Platonic metaphor of which she is fond, in the inner dialogue between Me and Myself. This has the implication, disconcerting for an age where uniformity is regarded as a hall-mark of truth, that no two thinking people will ever think quite alike. That is not to say that such thought is not communicable, or that individuals cannot learn from and stimulate one another: on the contrary, her own writings (and indeed the whole tradition of political thought) demonstrate that highly individual thinking can be articulated in accessible form, and that others can reflect upon it and assimilate it into their own thinking. This kind of thought is by no means arbitrary—if it were it would be of no interest to anyone else—but it is inescapably personal. The reflections of particular persons upon the political events of their time may be compared with the accounts given by different eye-witnesses of a battle. Their value will vary, according to their vantage-point, their vision, their previous experience of such situations, their preconceptions, and, of course, their ability; some accounts will be more illuminating than others; some may indeed be quite worthless. But to ask which is the *true* one, or to relapse into cynicism and say that, because they do not give identical accounts, there is no truth and everyone is entitled to think what he likes upon the matter, would obviously be misguided. It makes sense to ask of thinking like Hannah Arendt's whether and in what ways it is illuminating to the rest of us, and what experience it ignores or distorts; but to ask overall, 'Is it true?' or 'Can she prove it?', is beside the point.

Hannah Arendt's work, then, has the twofold significance for students of politics of being both a new and noteworthy example of political thought, and also a demonstration that that genre is by no means dead—a challenge to the social sciences that claim to have replaced it. Accordingly, this study has the twofold purpose of endeavouring to give an account of her work, and at the same time attempting to bring into focus some of the issues raised by the existence of that work at all, since it is consciously directed against most of the accepted academic trends of the present time. It may perhaps seem unnecessary for a secondary work to set out to elucidate an author's meaning while she is there to do it herself. However, although her books are not obscure in the sense in which, for instance, Hegel is obscure, they are difficult, because she has travelled far along unfamiliar pathways of thought, and what she has to say is subtle and complex. Students picking them up for the first time may well be bewildered; and while the only satisfactory remedy for that is rereading, some guidance may not be out of place. Her theories, being unusual and often polemical, are frequently open to objection. We shall therefore have occasion to consider criticisms of her work, and to attempt some very tentative assessments of the worth of her ideas.

One reason why Hannah Arendt's mode of thought is unfamiliar, and why many of her Anglo-Saxon readers may find her puzzling as well as exciting, is of course her own origin. Her intellectual background is Central European; and for all her discrimination in writing English it is easy to see in her books the signs of her education, with its much greater emphasis upon classical and historical studies than English or American education, and the influence of the German tradition of philosophy in which she grew up. In this study, however, we shall not be concerned directly with the sources of her thought, her relation to her intellectual background, or the development of her theory in response to other writers and circumstances. Interesting though such an inquiry would be, considerations of space make it impossible. In any case, as she herself is fond of pointing out, originality, the capacity of human beings to do or think something that could not have been foreseen, is always mysterious in its origins, and can never be exhausted by describing the circumstances of its birth. It is obviously relevant to her thinking that she is a Jew of German origin, that she inherited the rich culture of her country and was then obliged to emigrate: crucial, too, that she was brought face to face with totalitarianism, then with war, and finally with the problems of modern society in America. Her thought is concerned with these experiences, and her preoccupation with freedom certainly has much to do with the times in which she has lived. However, to try to explain her theory by reference to these influences and problems would be to miss precisely the salient point, that she is a person freely exercising her mind upon these problems, using this intellectual heritage in doing so. Others have been subject to identical influences and exposed to identical events without being prodded into thought by the *Zeitgeist*; others have contemplated tyranny without attempting a new understanding of freedom: and in searching for the 'sources' of a thinker's ideas one can all too easily overlook the central fact, the actual thinking mind. She has herself made a similar point in writing a Preface to the essays on various contemporaries published recently as *Men in Dark Times*;[4] and in view of the fact that the red thread running through all her thought is an affirmation of man's freedom against all attempts to reduce him to an automaton propelled by circumstances, it would be treason to the spirit of her work to endeavour to 'explain' it in any terms other than those of a thinking person reflecting upon the events of her age.

Just as political thought is often seen now as a primitive forerunner of political science, so originality is commonly thought of in scientific terms, as discovering or inventing something that was not known before, as Madame Curie discovered radium and James Watt invented the steam engine. It may perhaps be as well, therefore, to preface our discussion of Hannah Arendt by pointing out that originality need not and often does not consist in discovering new things, but in enabling us to notice things that were there all the time but that we overlooked because our attention was focused elsewhere. The example of visual perception may help to clarify this point. Professor Gombrich, in his richly illuminating book *Art and Illusion*,[5] has given many examples of the difficulty men have in taking in what is before their eyes, and their constant need for some schema to direct their attention and tell them what to look for. Once an artist has created such a schema, and shown us how something looks, we can see it easily ourselves; but our eyes are constantly influenced by the schema to which we are accustomed, so that we can only with difficulty break its spell and notice discrepancies. When the Chinese artist paints Derwentwater it turns out to look remarkably like a Chinese landscape; when the Gothicized draughtsman laboriously copies every detail of Chartres Cathedral, he fails to notice that one or two of the windows are, unexpectedly, Romanesque. Now, it is clear that visual perception is not the only aspect of experience that is dominated by our expectations and our conceptual vocabulary. Our conscious experience of everything around us, from the workings of our digestion to the behaviour of our friends, is affected by the categories we possess, the pigeon-holes in which experiences can be safely stored away to stop them vanishing from our consciousness. This is only noticeable when someone less ruled by existing categories than his fellows manages to create a new one—for then others find that the new pigeon-hole enables them to notice and recall all manner of experiences that formerly were forgotten because they had no name. An example of a category that liberated vast areas of previously unrecognized experience is the 'Unconscious', introduced into psychology and thence very rapidly into common discourse at the end of the last century. Like the physical conveniences of this technological age, it is hard to imagine how people ever did without it.

Originality, the introduction of new categories and ways of seeing things, or the replacement of an old set by a different one, is therefore illuminating in a precise sense: it highlights, brings out into the light of day, experiences that were previously not consciously regarded, with the paradoxical result that a writer can be highly original, and yet evoke from his readers the response: 'Yes, exactly, that is what I have always known, although I couldn't have expressed it before.' One of the functions of philosophers as of poets is to articulate experience in this way, to enable people to think consciously what they have been only half aware of, to give them names by which to remember experiences that would otherwise vanish without trace—and, as we shall see, much of Hannah Arendt's contribution to political theory is of this kind. Not the least important aspect of this activity is that it provides alternatives to the existing categories in terms of which we experience the world. This is very important. No one can provide new ways of seeing without challenging the old, and the greatest challenge to existing categories is simply the realization that they *are* categories, and not a simple transcription of reality. A European confronted by a Chinese landscape painting may not feel that it is a truer representation of reality than, say, the conventions of Constable: what he must realize, however, if he reflects upon the situation, is that the conventions he is accustomed to are conventions, and not simply reality as it presents itself. If one is confronted with two alternative conventions, one can no longer mistake one of them for simple reality.

Similarly in the case of political philosophy: Hannah Arendt's thought has the twofold quality we have described, both of providing articulations for experiences previously undescribed, and of challenging accepted ways of looking at the world by suggesting alternatives, so that whether or not her reader is prepared to accept her alternative as the truth, he must at any rate become consciously aware that he has been taking a great deal for granted. In what follows, we shall constantly have occasion to notice the thought-provoking effect of challenging existing categories and of drawing distinctions in new places; but one preliminary example may be given here. Hannah Arendt characterizes freedom as participation in public action among one's peers, the very opposite of the undisturbed private life that we usually think of when we use the term:

7

Freedom . . . is actually the reason that men live together in political organization at all. Without it, political life as such would be meaningless. The *raison d'être* of politics is freedom, and its field of experience is action.[6]

Where we ordinarily see freedom as the possession of the private individual, she sees it as something enjoyed in public; where we think of it as being let alone, she sees it as a concomitant of action among one's fellows. We shall be looking in detail later at her position and its justification; our point here is simply that, whether or not we can finally agree with her, she does make us realize that what we take for granted is not so obvious after all, and that there is another possible way of looking at things to be considered on its merits.

It is hardly possible to read Hannah Arendt's works without becoming aware of assumptions that we constantly make but that are clearly not self-evident. Her own highly individual manner of looking at human activity forces the unquestioned assumptions of the modern world into prominence by contrast and encourages us to re-examine them. To take an example at random: we are accustomed to regard 'natural' as a term of praise, 'artificial' as derogatory; we think of the evils of society as artificial, and imagine that we should be better off in a more natural environment. It startles us, therefore, to find Hannah Arendt reversing this order, identifying nature with necessity and exalting the specifically human capacity of artifice, which enables us to build a human world to live in instead of merely inhabiting the given world of nature like an animal. Her comment, for instance, upon the 'artificial' creation of the state of Israel is that it is precisely this artificiality that gives the Jewish achievement its human significance, although this is hard for a generation reared on doctrines of necessity to understand.[7]

Perhaps most startlingly, she proposes criteria of judgment and hierarchies of priority different from those commonly accepted, and articulates ideals almost unknown in the ordinary discourse of the modern world. In particular, she exalts the blessings of political action far above those pleasures of consumption that we are accustomed to regard as constituting a high standard of living. But whether or not one is prepared to go along with her transvaluation of values, it is illuminating

8

to become aware of the choice. Interestingly enough this side of her work has great affinities with what Max Weber, often regarded as the founder of modern value-free social science, saw as the proper task of academic inquiry. In the course of his tortuous and tormented reflections upon value-freedom and the limits of a science that could claim to be objective, Weber remarked that although no scientific inquiry can ever tell any-one what he ought to do, or relieve the individual of the burden of moral decision, nevertheless one of the functions of science in its effort to give a true description of reality, whether natural or social or political, is to articulate and elaborate the various possible values and their claims upon men: to describe faithfully the good things that human experience has dis-covered, not with a view to establishing a definitive hierarchy among them, still less of deriving from them rules for everyday life, but in order to shed light upon the choices that all men must make.[8] Hannah Arendt does not refer to Weber's dis-cussion, but her work can perhaps be characterized in his terms. As we shall see, she articulates vividly and persuasively blessings which are available to human experience, but which are at present almost completely forgotten.

While Hannah Arendt gives expression to many experiences that have previously lacked recognition, her reflections charac-teristically consist of articulating her subject-matter in the sense of spreading it out, making a great many distinctions, and thereby providing an unusually rich map of categories with which to chart experience. It is often characteristic of the categories of intellectual discourse that in pointing to what is held to be significant they leave out everything else: that is to say that they function as caricatures. Hobbes's theory, for instance, derives its enormous impact not least from its startling simplicity. Its power to illuminate human experience cannot be denied, but neither can the vast areas of which it takes no notice. Theories that are illuminating are often so by virtue of focusing attention on one thing to the exclusion of all else. But Hannah Arendt's challenge to existing ways of thought is presented not in terms of greater simplicity than these, but by means of a theory of greater complexity and richness. Not the least of her heterodoxies is that she provides us with the means of making many more distinctions than we ordinarily use our language for, and shows us why it is important to make them. In order to do so, she does not find it necessary to follow Bentham's example by inventing her own terms and trying to bring them into use: instead she manages to find within our existing language more shades of meaning than we are commonly aware of when we use different words as synonyms. Her claim is that the very existence of all these different terms testifies that the experiences they describe were known to our forefathers, even if we have ceased to notice them. One of her main quarrels with modern academics, and with social scientists in particular, is their lack of sensitivity to words, and their replacement of a rich language, full of precise shades of meaning, with a narrow jargon lacking in existential resonance. As we shall see, her arguments constantly hinge upon linguistic distinctions, some of them strained but some undoubtedly illuminating.

One striking feature of her work is her use of history, particularly Greek and Roman history. She uses it not merely to provide vivid illustrations, but, much more crucially, as the means of finding an Archimedean point outside the present to which she can appeal against the modern world and its assumptions. Her knowledge of history, and of the mode of life and scale of priorities preserved in the ancient languages, enables her to draw upon a wider range of human experience than we are now commonly aware of. Immersed in our own moment of time, we take for granted, for instance, that the highest Good in life is to be happy, that happiness is to be found in a high standard of living, and that the proper object of social and political arrangements is to provide such a standard. This seems so obvious that it comes as a shock when Hannah Arendt points out how very recent and unusual in human culture such a scale of priorities is: that the Greeks and the Romans, and even the men of the American Revolution in the eighteenth century, knew nothing of it, and that the blessings which life held for them were of a quite different kind; that, for instance, participation in public affairs and the pursuit of glory were things good in themselves, to which the possession of a bodily sufficiency was only a means. Her implicit claim is that the potential range of human experience does not change much—these same blessings are still possible, and are sometimes rediscovered by accident when men are driven by circumstances into public life, as in the French Resistance during the war against Hitler : but where articulate culture gives them no named and recognized place among the good things of life, the experiences are quickly forgotten even by those who had them, and are not communicated to others.[9] Throughout her works the conviction is manifest that men in the modern world are depriving themselves of most of what can make human life worth living, as a result of having forgotten and ceased to have names for the treasured experiences of their forefathers.

Her use of history, therefore, is as a repository of human experience in which we can find permanent human possibilities that are wider than those known and expected within our own culture. History, and above all the records of Greek and Roman antiquity, provides a court of appeal against the present. One might perhaps expect, in view of this historical-mindedness, that she would see herself as standing within the great tradition of political thought, and trying to recall to its inheritance a world that has almost forgotten it. However, the radicalism of her appeal to history goes much further than that : for she appeals not only against the narrowness of modern culture, but also against the tradition of political thought itself, which she sees as being quite largely responsible for restricting the field of articulate human experience to its present scope. Her point here is that ever since its beginning with Plato, the Western tradition of political thought has been a philosopher's tradition, and thereby in some ways actually anti-political. The advent of Christianity, with its other-worldliness, merely confirmed this trend. The building up of a tradition of thinking about politics, and the formation of a vocabulary which has passed into common speech, were done by men whose priorities were directly opposed to those of political life : who were concerned with contemplation rather than action, with penetrating to eternal truth rather than with performing immortal deeds, and who lived in the mental solitude of the philosopher or the saint, not in the public arena of the man of action. As a result the political vocabulary inherited by Western culture has been a curiously unpolitical one. In particular she considers that our understanding of

freedom has been strangely distorted, for instead of the freedom of the free citizen in action among his peers and able to
initiate common enterprises, what has become embodied in the
term and our traditional understanding of it is the freedom of
the private individual to withdraw into his own self and be
unconditioned from outside:

Since the whole problem of freedom arises for us in the horizon
of Christian traditions on one hand, and of an originally anti-
political philosophic tradition on the other, we find it difficult to
realize that there may exist a freedom which is not an attribute of the
will but an accessory of doing and acting.[10]

Her claim is, then, that because the traditional understanding
of politics has been formed by philosophers, who were reflective and articulate, rather than by the men of action themselves, the experiences of the latter have been largely unex-
pressed and forgotten, and even those who have rediscovered
them, like the men of the American Revolution or the French
Resistance, have had difficulty in recognizing what they found,
or of naming it so as to preserve its remembrance.

Her attitude to the tradition of political thought is therefore
ambivalent. On the one hand, she is herself a student of it, and
her reflections often form themselves around some idea or
remark of Plato, Hobbes, Locke and the others (although in
the course of using and extending their ideas she is inclined to
be somewhat cavalier in her interpretations [11]). On the other
hand she makes the remarkably radical claim that the tradition consists largely of misinterpretations of political experience, and appeals beyond it to the recorded experience of
men of affairs like Jefferson and Adams in the American
Revolution, or Cicero in the Roman Republic, or the Greeks
as expressed in the poetry, the drama, the history and the
language of Athens. Since the tradition itself is misleading,
reactions and reversals within it seem to her less significant
than the gulf between the tradition as a whole and political
experience itself. She sees Marx as ending the tradition by
turning it and its priorities upside-down, by defining man in
terms of labour instead of reason, and exalting action in the
place of thought: but since he merely turned the existing categories upside-down, she considers that he still missed the point

of political action, for there was no articulation of its peculiar qualities existing in the tradition. Whether she herself succeeds in escaping from the shackles of theory to grasp the reality of action is of course a moot point, which we shall take up later.

Hannah Arendt's works of political thought cannot be identified with any particular party or group. The best known of her books is probably her account and critique of totalitarianism, by which term she refers to the regimes of Hitler and Stalin, but the standpoint of her critique is neither liberalism nor neo-Marxism. She has considerable respect for Marx (with whom, indeed, she seems to engage in a continuous dialogue) but is quite without enthusiasm for his doctrines and those of his followers, which indeed seem to her to be typical of modern intellectual trends that are equally visible in the liberalism and social science of the West. Her philosophy, therefore, while certainly anti-Marxist, cannot be categorized as 'liberal' or 'Western', since all the various opposing ideologies and intellectual orthodoxies of the modern world seem to her to have a great deal in common, and to be all deplorable, although beside the fruit of the totalitarian ideologies the others pale into comparative insignificance. These common trends that she deplores will become clear as we proceed with the examination of her thought: but their common core is that men under their spell experience themselves not as free beings but as automata moved and dominated by processes; as atoms within a mass whose movements are predictable; as existing only to produce, consume and pass away like animals; as living within a stream of history determined by forces over which they have no control. Against this self-experience of modern man, she reasserts the understanding of man as a free agent, who is capable of building a permanent human world amid the flux of nature, who can think freely and create for himself an understanding of the world, and who is above all capable of *acting*, of taking the initiative and doing things in company with his fellows, thereby releasing purely human power and breaking out of the treadmill of meaningless and predictable behaviour. An example (according to her interpretation) [12] of action of this kind is the Hungarian Revolution of 1956; and it is one which, despite its failure, is a great joy to her because it shows that in spite of the pressures of the modern world, at their most intense in totalitarianism, men are still capable of seizing their fate in both hands. It seems to her typical of those social sciences which systematize the loss of human significance in the modern world that their dearest wish is to be able to predict the future, whereas a genuinely significant event like the Hungarian Revolution, unlike dull years of endurance of tyranny, can of course never be predicted.

Her attitudes to current political issues cannot be fitted neatly into the customary categories of Right and Left. Of her opposition to Marxism and to the U.S.S.R. there can be no doubt, and as a result she is commonly regarded in Leftist circles as being Right-wing. Certain elements within her thought give colour to this classification. For instance, she reasserts the importance of private property (although her views on this point, when further examined, turn out to give little comfort to conservatives); and one of her books, *On Revolution*, is organized round an elaborate contrast between the American Revolution, for which she has great admiration, and the French Revolution, which she regards as an unqualified disaster. Again, there is a Nietzschean strain within her work of distrust for the masses and their effect on politics, and her attitudes are élitist, although hardly in the sense of endorsing any existing ruling class. Her central theme, the exaltation of political freedom over concern for the standard of living, might strike most socialists as being Right-wing. However, if a case can be made from the socialist point of view for calling her Right-wing, any self-respecting Rightist would repudiate her for the revolutionary tone of much of her work. She certainly cannot be considered an apologist for contemporary America, which she regards as having largely forgotten its own inheritance of freedom; her interpretation of freedom itself has a lot more in common with Rosa Luxemburg than with John Stuart Mill; while her very élitism is a matter of wishing politics to rest in the hands, not of any traditional political class, but rather of those, whatever their origin, who have the courage and public spirit to emerge from private life and take responsibility among their fellows. It seems to her that in the last hundred years those who have belonged to this category have usually been militant members of the working class, and she is filled with admiration for the Paris Communards and the founders of the Russian Soviets. As her recent book *On Violence* (prompted by the troubles in America) shows, she has considerable sympathy with the participatory ideals of the student movement and their disdain for the Establishment, though none with their rhetoric of violence and destruction. Her political standpoint cannot even be characterized without qualification as 'Jewish', for her writings on the Middle Eastern situation, and particularly her book on the trial of Eichmann, have involved her in bitter controversy with other Jewish writers. She has even been accused of being anti-Jewish, and of having tried to exculpate Eichmann. Nonsensical as these charges must appear to anyone who reads her book without prejudice they do make the point that she can hardly be regarded as a partisan. If any label at all were to be pinned on her, it could only be 'Republican'—not in the sense of the American party, but in the old, eighteenth-century sense of a partisan of public freedom, a companion of men like de Tocqueville, Jefferson and Machiavelli.

Like most original thinkers, she has developed a mode of thought which, although it is not a system and her ideas have developed and changed from one book to another, is nevertheless a fairly coherent structure within which the terms she uses and the ideas she puts forward take on special meanings and constantly refer to and illuminate one another. Her most comprehensive and fundamental work is *The Human Condition*, and we shall be devoting a large part of our attention to that: but the ideas she puts forward in it are extended and qualified in *On Revolution* and in her many essays. These general reflections, however, were preceded by and followed from her attempt to come to grips with the most critical phenomenon of our time, her book on *The Origins of Totalitarianism*; and it is with this that we propose to deal first.

2

Totalitarianism

'. . . totalitarianism differs essentially from other forms of political oppression known to us such as despotism, tyranny and dictatorship.' [1]

The Origins of Totalitarianism, Hannah Arendt's first major political work, is also the one for which she is most widely known and has been both highly praised and much criticized. It is an extremely complex and idiosyncratic book, and we cannot hope here either to do justice to the subtlety of its argument or to discuss all the objections that can be raised against it. We can only attempt to consider the purpose and method of Hannah Arendt's treatment of totalitarianism, and look at some of the more fundamental criticisms that can be made of it.

Perhaps the first point to bear in mind when approaching *The Origins of Totalitarianism* is the time at which it was written —as Hannah Arendt herself points out in the Introduction to the third edition. It was first published in 1951, and written under the impact of the horrors of Nazism in Germany and Stalinism in Russia. It is not a detached attempt by a political scientist to define a form of political system in the abstract, with a view to its use in future classifications; neither is it an academic historian's analysis of a recognized phenomenon— of the type, for instance, of some ingenious new account of the origins of the English Civil War. It is rather an attempt to understand, to get an intellectual grip upon, the appalling and incomprehensible experiences that Hannah Arendt's genera- tion had been through, and to make intelligible what seemed simply nightmarish. At the centre of this nightmare were the Nazi concentration camps, and it is these above all that mean totalitarianism to Hannah Arendt and about which she set out to answer the question, how could this have happened? It is obvious throughout the book that she was thinking primarily of Nazism in writing it, as the prominent place she gives to racism makes clear. However, she talks throughout of 'totalitarianism' as a general phenomenon, including both Stalinism and Nazism, and her model is a conflation of features of both regimes. As we shall see later, this is one of the points on which her book has been most plausibly criticized; but however misleading it may in some respects be to try to equate the two political systems, it is important to remember that, different though their ideologies were, both gave rise to nightmarish terror—in lumping them together Hannah Arendt was seizing on something that is specifically modern and trying to understand how it could have come about. The Nazi death camps are the paradigm of totalitarianism, with Stalin's purges paralleling them in a colossal wickedness that defies common-sense understanding. Hannah Arendt sets out in her book to characterize as totalitarianism the social and political context into which the camps fit and in which alone they make any kind of sense—and to trace back into European history and culture the elements which made totalitarianism possible. Her book is organized on the principle of convergence, starting with these elements, in two massive sections on antisemitism and imperialism, and gathering them together into her characterization of totalitarianism in the final section. However, since her argument is intricate it will be easier to summarize in reverse, starting with her description of totalitarianism and going back from that to what she sees as its sources.

THE TOTALITARIAN MODEL

In the second edition of her book, Hannah Arendt added a concluding chapter in which she attempted to sum up what differentiated totalitarianism from older and more familiar forms of tyranny; it will be convenient to take this summing-up as our starting-point. The chapter is entitled 'Ideology and Terror', for it seems to her that the peculiar horror of totalitarianism lies in the fact that the cruelties it perpetrates on such an unprecedented scale are not even intelligible in any other than ideological terms. They are not the outcome of undisciplined fury (compare the massacre of the Jews, carefully organized and recorded in bureaucratic detail, with, for instance, the massacres committed by the Mongol invaders of the Middle Ages) : yet neither do these cruelties serve the utilitarian interests of those who carry them out (the Nazis actually endangered their war effort by diverting valuable resources to the ferrying of Jews to extermination camps). They are colossally systematic and organized, and yet they make no sense at all except in terms of an ideology that seems utterly fictitious to all but its adherents. According to Hannah Arendt, what distinguished totalitarian domination from the tyranny of innumerable historical despots was not merely the scale of its mass murders but the fact that these were understood and carried out as the rational putting into practice of a doctrine according to which, for instance, race struggles were a law of nature, and considerations of freedom of choice on the part of the executioners or innocence and guilt on the part of the victims were entirely beside the point. What strikes her as new, appalling and in need of explanation about Nazism and Stalinism is the robot-like behaviour of both victims and executioners, both evidently feeling that they had no choice, no opportunity for action, in going through their ritual, but were merely obeying forces greater than human wills. She remarks that previous tyrannies have, almost by definition, been lawless examples of arbitrary will on the part of the rulers, whereas precisely the point about totalitarianism is its denial of any place for human will in a world where everything is determined by laws of nature or history. Individual human wishes, intentions and actions are irrelevant to the struggle of races or classes, for Jews or kulaks are doomed to die not because of anything they may have done or thought but because of what they are. Within the realm of ideology all actions, however appalling, are merely deductions from the accepted premises and follow logically, however crazy they may seem to common sense. Thus, while from the point of view of even the most cynical common sense the systematic annihilation of the Jews was quite insane, from the point of view of Nazi ideology it simply followed from the theory of racial supremacy and was a natural and inevitable deduction. It is this very consistency which, like the relentless logic of a paranoiac who can explain everything that happens as part of the conspiracy against him, seems so weird to the outside observer. What Hannah Arendt wishes to pin down is this nightmare quality of totalitarianism, in which madness could strike whole nations, and millions be systematically murdered for the sake of consistency with an ideological system : and what seems to her to demand explanation is how it could have come about that so many men could be so detached from any restraint of common sense as to be able to conceive such projects, carry them out, or even suffer them without resistance.

Ideology and terror seem to her to constitute the essence of totalitarianism thought about in the abstract; in the third section of her book she attempts a more concrete characterization of this new political phenomenon, drawing in some detail on the experience of both Nazism and Stalinism. She begins with the point that in spite of the unprecedented criminality of both regimes, Nazism and Stalinism were remarkable for their mass support and the selflessness and devotion of their adherents. Instead of the cynical, self-seeking brigands whom one might expect (and who could indeed be found at the head of the movements) the ranks were filled by men who were prepared to identify themselves wholly with their cause, to sacrifice not only themselves but their friends, family and principles for it, and even, in the Russian case, to oblige their rulers with false confessions of their own guilt. Alongside this amazing devotion, Hannah Arendt sets the equally odd phenomenon, in the case of the Nazis, of the devotion disappearing the moment its object was removed. One moment Germany was full of fanatical Nazis, the next the idealism seemed to have vanished completely and there were no martyrs ready to die for the lost cause. The two phenomena seem to her to be related and to indicate that totalitarian movements were not movements of classes, bound together by real, permanent, objective interests, but of *masses*—of people who no longer belonged to a class or to any other group, and instead shared only the experience of being superfluous in the world, having no reason for their existence. She distinguishes between the 'masses' and the 'mob'. By the latter she means the socially disreputable, the outcasts and criminal elements, and she notes that the leaders of the Nazi and Bolshevik movements were drawn from this band of adventurers accustomed to war against established society. By the masses, on the contrary, she means people who would in any stable society be perfectly content to fill the role to which they were born, but who found themselves cut off, isolated from their fellows, convinced of their own helplessness and unimportance, and prepared to devote themselves to any organization that gave them a place in the world and a reason for existing.

Totalitarian movements, she claims, characteristically organize masses of atomized, isolated individuals, demanding their total loyalty regardless not only of other claims but even of their own convictions, since they are expected to follow the party line whatever bewildering changes may be dictated by the leader. She goes on to discuss their use of propaganda, concentrating on Nazism. Nazi propaganda, she says, was not misleading in the manner of public relations—a matter of attractive lies intended to cover sinister interests: it was, instead, a statement of the real aims of the movement, which attracted the German masses, but which was at the same time ignored by outsiders because it seemed contrary to common sense and to the material interests of the Nazis themselves. Because Nazism did not appeal to or cater for the interests either of the party or of the masses, its rise and attractions seemed incomprehensible to outsiders, who were taken unprepared by Hitler's rise to power and by his policies; but this anti-utilitarianism seems to Hannah Arendt to be explicable in terms of the psychology of masses. She remarks that interest is relevant in politics only where individuals belong to stable social groups that have clear collective interests. Individual interests are too diverse to be caught in the net of a party programme where, as in the case of modern masses, the individuals belong to no collective body and can identify themselves with no collective interests.

Totalitarian propaganda consists largely of prediction, and is prepared to change the world to make its statements come true; it deals also in secret conspiracies which it has detected, and through its ideology presents an account of the world that uncovers the hidden meaning of experience, providing its adherents with a total explanation. The attractiveness of this sort of propaganda seems to Hannah Arendt to be part and parcel of the loss by modern masses of their hold on reality.

People now, according to her, tend to trust their own experience, their eyes and ears, less than a system which by virtue of its consistency is more rational than reality. Just as real life contains coincidences that no novelist would dare put into a book because they would seem so improbable, so the constant fortuitousness of reality makes it less convincing than the perfect consistency of ideological fictions, in which everything fits. She explains this mass flight from reality into fiction by reference to the experience of masses in this century—an experience of disorder, rapid change, political and economic collapse, chaotic happenings which undermined the stable social relations necessary to sustain common sense and enable us to distinguish what is plausible from what is not. The willingness of the Bolsheviks to sign false confessions, to deny their own knowledge of their innocence for the sake of ideological consistency, seems to her an example of this phenomenon of atomized mass-man's separation from reality and his dependence upon a world of fiction. According to her the specific content of Nazi propaganda was also geared to the needs of mass-man. There was nothing original about anti-semitism, but in actually making proof of non-Jewish blood a qualification for party membership the Nazis provided their members with a means of self-definition as a master race, so that the most ordinary Nazi gained a feeling not only of belonging, but of belonging to an élite.

Whereas the content of the propaganda of the totalitarian movements had nothing original about it, the organization of the movements seems to her to be new. This novelty consists in the onion-like structure whereby the party is surrounded by front organizations and sympathizers, while within the party militant groups like the S.A. and S.S. in Nazism are distinguished from ordinary members. This provides a graduation of militancy from the centre to the outside world, and acts as a kind of shock-absorber preventing outsiders from realizing how radical the movement is (since they only come into contact with sympathizers) and the real militants from realizing how monstrous their beliefs and actions are (since they are surrounded by a world of less extreme party members who represent 'normality' to them). Hannah Arendt remarks on the way in which this hierarchy of initiation supports the movement's ideological fiction and public lies through a variable mixture of gullibility and cynicism. This mixture, she says, is characteristic of masses:

In an ever-changing, incomprehensible world the masses had reached the point where they would, at the same time, believe everything and nothing, think that everything was possible and that nothing was true.[2]

People can be made to believe the most fantastic statement one day, and the next day, if its falsehood is proved, will take refuge in cynicism, protesting that they had known all along that their leaders were lying for tactical purposes. Public statements are intended to be swallowed only by the outer group of sympathizers: the inner circles recognize them as lies and admire their leaders, despising the uninitiated for their naïveté, so that what Hannah Arendt calls a 'hierarchy of contempt' exists within the movement. The inner élite does not even believe in the official ideology, so that such a startling volte-face as the alliance between Hitler and Stalin leaves them quite unmoved.

Having discussed the nature of a totalitarian mass movement (clearly with reference more to Nazism than to Stalinism) Hannah Arendt goes on to consider totalitarianism in power. Rise to power in one particular country is bound to create problems for a totalitarian movement because its fictitious world of ideology and propaganda, its disregard for facts, becomes more difficult to maintain: power means a direct confrontation with the real world, and tends always to dilute ideology, stabilize radical movements, and generally normalize those who capture it. It was expected in the outside world that power would have this effect upon the Nazis and Bolsheviks; but this expectation was disappointed, and the two movements, according to Hannah Arendt, retained their nature and remained in a state of motion by regarding the country in which they had seized power not as their final goal but as merely a base for global conquest and a laboratory in which to carry out experiments in total domination. She considers that the shapelessness of government in Germany and Russia was deliberate, part and parcel of the nature of mass movements in that there was nothing so stable as an established hierarchy, but instead only rule by the will of the leader, manifested through whatever organ he happened to choose at a particular time. Again, totalitarian rule differs from normal states, even despotic ones, in being unconcerned with considerations of utility. In the case of Nazism, it was when the political situation was becoming more and more desperate, as the danger of losing the war loomed closer, that the Nazis became most fanatical in implementing their ideology, at the cost of much more obviously vital military considerations. Her point is that to think of totalitarian rulers within the traditional political terms, and to try to understand them, for instance, simply as particularly ruthless players of the game of power politics, is completely misleading: they are not in fact playing that game at all, since they are not concerned with the national interest of their countries, or indeed with the calculable consequences of their actions, but only with their world of ideological fictions. Hence the extreme unpredictability of their actions, and the difficulty that ordinary politicians, versed in the ordinary ways of power politics, have in dealing with them.

In totalitarian states, the state authority is only a façade behind which real power belongs to the secret police, whose activity actually increases as the apparent need for them, to combat internal opposition, ceases to exist. It is when all actual opposition is destroyed that police power comes into its own, with the aim of establishing total domination. Hannah Arendt considers that both Hitler in Germany and Stalin in Russia shared this aim. Instead of seeking out real enemies of the régime—people opposed to it openly or in secret—as familiar despots do, the totalitarian ruler goes one better by attacking 'objective enemies': people who, like the Jews in Germany or the kulaks in Russia, are held to be enemies by definition, not because of what they as individuals may be doing or thinking. It seems to Hannah Arendt that the attempt at total domination and the notion of the 'objective enemy' is much more fundamental in both cases than the particular content of the category. The Nazis went on from the Jews to the Poles, who were next in line for extermination, and had plans for disposing of 'racially unfit' Germans; Stalin proceeded from kulaks to Tartars, former prisoners of war, etc. In all these cases, what a man might have done or thought was not even pretended to be the reason for his fate: he must suffer or die simply because he fell into a particular category defined by the leader.

This consistent arbitrariness negates human freedom more efficiently than any tyranny ever could. One had at least to be an enemy of tyranny in order to be punished by it. Freedom of opinion was not abolished for those who were brave enough to risk their necks. Theoretically, the choice of opposition remains in totalitarian regimes too; but such freedom is almost invalidated if committing a voluntary act only assures a 'punishment' that everyone else may have to bear anyway.[3]

Hannah Arendt comes finally to consider the concentration and extermination camps which she sees as the central feature of totalitarianism, and which she interprets as laboratories in which the totalitarian rulers prove that everything is possible, that human beings can be reduced to mere identical bundles of reactions and their personalities, freedom and spontaneity eradicated. Total domination, she says, 'strives to organize the infinite plurality and differentiation of human beings as if all humanity were just one individual'.[4] This aim, which was achieved among the élite by indoctrination, is achieved against the victims in the camps by terror. She writes vividly of the problems involved in describing or even in remembering the experience of the concentration camps. So like a nightmare was this, so completely contrary to common sense, that once it has ceased the victims themselves find it hard to believe that it was real. The camps, fulfilling no utilitarian function, conforming to no economic interest, had this air of unreality: everything done in them was known from the realms of sadistic fantasy, or from visions of hell, but it was difficult for everyone concerned to believe that what was happening was real. She describes the destruction of personality systematized in the camps. The victims first ceased to exist as juridical persons, since they were placed outside the law, deprived of all rights, in a much worse position than a criminal who is charged with a specific offence which carries a specific sentence. Nor could they exist as moral persons, since choice was made meaningless by the arbitrary nature of the

terror. There was none of the publicity necessary for martyr-
dom to be meaningful, and in any case, those who did try to
fight back jeopardized their friends and relations. The Nazis
did their best, through conditions in the camps, to destroy
individual personality as well, and they succeeded to the
extent that most of the victims had so far lost the possibility of
action that very few of them ever made any attempt to resist
death.

It seems to Hannah Arendt that the concentration camps,
for all their apparent lack of comprehensible utility, were in
fact highly functional in totalitarianism, forming a testing
ground for radical social possibilities, a training in domination
for the élite and a source of terror to overawe the rest of the
population. They were therefore an essential means of establishing total power, of eliminating all freedom and spontaneity.
In demonstrating the superfluity of human beings and the
senselessness of their existence they reflected the experience of
modern masses; but at the same time this senselessness,
including the existence of the camps, was explained quite
logically in the supersense of the totalitarian ideology.

This, then, in very bald summary, is Hannah Arendt's model
of totalitarianism, of which she regards Nazi Germany and
Stalin's Russia as the two examples to date.

All these characteristics, the senselessness, the contempt for
reality, the lack of freedom and enslavement to fiction, seem to
Hannah Arendt to reflect the experience of masses in our time :
the central experience of 'loneliness',[5] of being uprooted, being
superfluous, having no recognized place among others in a common world, and consequently having no common sense shared
with others to establish what is real and what imagined, what is
reasonable and what absurd. She remarks that the only human
capacity that can function perfectly in this kind of isolation is
the capacity for logical reasoning from a premise to its conclusions, and it seems to her that ideological thinking exempli-
fies this capacity unrestrained by the necessary check of a
common sense of reality. She quotes a remark of Luther's to the
effect that a lonely man 'always deduces one thing from the
other and thinks everything to the worst'. Men, she thinks, are
prepared for totalitarian domination by an experience of
loneliness more widespread in our time than ever before.

As we shall see later, much of her political thinking is concerned with matters which arise out of her understanding of totalitarianism: notably with freedom, understood as the power of individuals to act together and to originate; with the conflict between reality and fiction, and the dependence of a sense of reality, common sense, on a stable community; and with the human attempt to achieve total domination, to accept nothing as given, exemplified in totalitarianism on the one hand and in moon races, for example, on the other. These seem to her the political problems of our time. Before looking at her treatment of them, however, we must return to her attempt to understand the origins of this phenomenon that she has characterized as totalitarian: how could it have come about?

THE ORIGINS OF TOTALITARIANISM

She has herself written (in a reply to a review of her book by Eric Voegelin) [6] about the problems involved in trying to answer this question, and has emphasized that her book is not meant to be a history of totalitarianism, but rather a tracing of the elements that crystallized into it. Her emphasis is less on particular historical events in Germany and Russia than on general political developments like imperialism and the institutional changes that accompanied it; on general social developments like the growth of antisemitism; and on modes of thought such as racism. However, her purpose is not simply to list factors which, put together, produced totalitarianism, but rather to show by means of a consideration of these things the kind of experiences people were living through that made totalitarian ways of thinking and behaving possible. For instance, in her study of imperialism she is concerned not only with the institutional fact that the rapid expansion of empire in the late nineteenth century made rule by the arbitrary decree of officials normal procedure even where, as in the British Empire, a tradition of constitutional government existed, but also with the experience of uprooted Europeans finding themselves at the other side of the world among strange, and, in Africa, primitive peoples, and realizing that their conventional ideas of what it is reasonable or sane to do *were* conventional and that there are no limits other than convention to what is possible. It is experiences of this sort that Hannah Arendt is trying to pin down, precisely because the aspects of totalitarianism that cry out for explanation are less a matter of institutions than of attitudes. Given the resources of modern governments, the murder of millions of Jews and Russian peasants was feasible enough: but how could anyone conceive or carry out such projects? How could people see them as possible or reasonable things to do? Because she is trying to understand this problem of attitudes, she endeavours to penetrate to experiences preceding and underlying them; and because experiences can only be identified where they have been articulated she constantly draws upon the literature of her period for these articulations. In her accounts of antisemitism and imperialism, for instance, she draws on the writings of Disraeli and Proust in the former case, Conrad, Kipling and T. E. Lawrence in the latter. This dependence on literary evidence, and indeed her whole method, is unorthodox, and we shall have occasion later to consider the objections to which it lies open; it is important, however, to realize in approaching her account why she adopts such a method.

Her argument is exceedingly intricate, since she does a great many things simultaneously. Her book contains fairly straightforward historical accounts of certain phenomena, for instance of antisemitism and racialist theories. It also contains discussions of political phenomena such as the role of Jews in the nation-state, the imperialist expansion of the late nineteenth century, government by officials, etc., all of which form strands woven into her understanding of what made totalitarianism possible. It contains brilliantly written *vignettes* of individuals like Disraeli or Lawrence whom she sees as representatives of particularly significant experiences; and it is tied together by a collection of key concepts, notably that of 'superfluousness', that run like red threads through the narrative. However, in the course of her treatment of these various themes, she develops a central argument concerned with the polarities of the nation-state on the one hand and the individual on the other. Put very baldly, this is that totalitarianism was made possible on the one hand by the destruction of the nation-state with its stable legal and territorial structure in favour of

imperialist expansion, and on the other hand by a complementary tendency for individuals to identify themselves not as
citizens or members of a class but as representatives of much
more nebulous entities such as races, distinguished from others
by innate qualities. We shall see how she develops this argument in the course of her account of antisemitism and
imperialism, and how it forms one of many interconnections
holding the book together.

The first section of her book is concerned with antisemitism,
and she starts by asking why it was that Nazis made antisemitism so much the centre of their totalitarian experiment:
why was hostility to the Jews so important? Surely it was not
merely accidental that they were seized on as the scapegoats
for resentment? She tries to explain this choice of Jews as the
victims of Nazism by suggesting that the Jews were in a
peculiar and crucial relationship to the state on the one hand
and the circles of high society on the other. She suggests that
politically the attack on the Jews was part of a much wider
attack on the framework of the nation-state, in which the
Jews had held a crucial position, and that socially it followed
from the role that the Jews themselves had adopted in order to
overcome social discrimination.

We shall have occasion later to criticize Hannah Arendt's
discussion of the nation-state, chiefly because of the difficulty
of finding out to which actual states she means the term to
refer. She claims that the nation states of Western Europe had
in their classic period been built upon a precarious balance of
classes, such that the state itself—government, legal structure
and bureaucracy—stood above the warring classes and the
parties that represented them. The Jews resembled the state
machinery in not belonging to any class, and they also stood in
a special relation to the state in that they were both used by
governments, as bankers and agents, and protected by governments against the hostility of the people. They habitually lived
under special laws which were a mixture of privileges and
restrictions. In the multi-national Austro-Hungarian monarchy they were again identified with the state, which stood
above the mutually hostile nationalities. Consequently they
were a natural target for attack by all groups, classes in the
nation-state or nationalities in Austria-Hungary, that turned

against the state, and Hannah Arendt suggests that, ironically enough, it was at the end of the nineteenth century, just when the Jews were in fact losing their previously dominant financial and political position, that anti-state groups arose and attacked them, accusing them of wielding vast secret influence. Politically, then, antisemitism seems to her to be part and parcel of a revolutionary attack upon the classic state structure, a movement which she examines in her section on imperialism. Antisemitism was, however, not only a political matter but a social one as well, and it was the social element that gave it its bitterness. This element she tries to pin down in an intricate argument, drawing heavily on the writings of Disraeli and Proust. She is concerned with the ambiguities of being Jewish in the nineteenth century, when, with the spread of greater social mobility, there was an increasing quest for social integration by certain Jews. They wished to be accepted by polite society as ordinary persons, but they found that their only claim on society's notice was their oddity, the fact that they were different, exotic, Jewish. The attempt to be like everyone else led them into subtly stressing their differences, and Hannah Arendt is vivid upon the torments of this ambiguous situation, which did indeed give rise to a characteristic personality in those who suffered it. They found themselves obliged to insist upon their specific Jewishness in order to gain acceptance; antisemitism retorted in kind by regarding Jewishness as an innate quality. In the decadent circles of society in France in the 1890s or Germany in the 1920s, Jews were fashionable *because* they were regarded as disreputable, like homosexuals: they had the fascination of vice, and were interesting because of their sinister aura. Consequently they both became a symbol of the corruption of society to those outside it, and also represented for members of society a kind of secret vice of which they then cleansed themselves by becoming viciously antisemitic. Hannah Arendt describes this process taking place in France through the ramifications of the Dreyfus Affair, but emphasizes what a distance there is between the antisemitism of the affair, vicious though it was, and full-scale Nazism. She claims that the crucial difference lies in the fact that the affair took place within the framework of an intact nation-state, so that the social antisemitism was not given final momentum by the explosive political forces that were attacking the nation-state structure and the Jews with it. It is these forces that she goes on to describe in her section on imperialism.

This section is the most elaborate part of her book, and contains some of the most brilliant and at the same time some of the most questionable of her ideas. Her argument is, very baldly, that totalitarianism followed from the reintroduction to Europe of political trends that had been formed and exported during the great imperialist expansion of the late nineteenth century. This expansion destroyed the old cohesion and political forms of the nation-state, while providing in racism a new way of holding together masses of detached people, and in administrative rule—'Bureaucracy'— a new way of governing them. She finds the direct ancestors of totalitarianism in Germany and Russia in the Pan-German and Pan-Slav movements, which she regards as having, in the absence of overseas possessions, exemplified in Europe the trends that Britain and France confined to their empires. As we shall see, it is an essential part of her argument that imperialism, racism and such movements as Pan-Germanism and Pan-Slavism were in no sense extensions of nationalism, but were directly opposed to and hostile to it.

The first characteristic of imperialism that seems to her to foreshadow totalitarianism and be destructive of the nation-state is simply its drive towards continual expansion, expansion for its own sake. This characteristic, typical of capitalist business undertakings, seems to her to be a consequence of the introduction into politics of purposes and ways of thinking that were really entirely economic, concerned with profits, investments and balance sheets, while the political expansion of empire was merely a matter of the flag following trade, and power being extended to protect ever-increasing investments. Since the purposes of expansion were purely economic, not political, there was no attempt to found new bodies politic in the overseas possessions: the only aspects of the state that were exported were the instruments of power, the army, the police and the bureaucracy. These were vastly expanded, unrestrained by any political control in the overseas territories, and this precedent of rule by force without any other political cement was, according to Hannah Arendt, to be reimported into Europe later. She attributes the curiously a-political phenomenon of an expansion conceived purely in economic terms, with power used instrumentally, to the political dominance of the bourgeoisie. She maintains that the classic nation-state had stood above and detached from the conflict of economic classes mainly because the dominant class, the bourgeoisie, had been more interested in its private business affairs than in wielding political power. She calls imperialism 'the political emancipation of the bourgeoisie', claiming that it was the risks of overseas investment that at last led the bourgeoisie, in the latter years of the nineteenth century, to concern themselves with matters of state—but to do so in a purely instrumental way, a way which was in fact destructive of politics. Unlimited expansion, however much sense it might make in business, could if conceived as the endless expansion of power lead only to totalitarianism. In a brilliant but extremely questionable essay in interpretation she presents Hobbes, the philosopher of the endless pursuit of 'power after power', as setting out the principles of a bourgeois politics which did not become fully realized until more than two hundred years after his death.

By means of imperialist expansion, capital that had become superfluous in Europe was exported—and so also were the superfluous men thrown up by capitalism, the mob of those whom economic advance had deprived of their position in society. This class of the superfluous were in the case of England exported to the empire— one of the main reasons why otherwise enlightened Englishmen supported imperialism— but in Germany, Austria and Russia, where there were no substantial overseas possessions to send them to, such men had perforce to stay at home, and become according to Hannah Arendt the raw material of the proto-totalitarian movements, Pan-Germanism and Pan-Slavism. She makes great play with the notion of superfluousness—superfluous capital, superfluous men, exported to South Africa in particular in pursuit of the superfluous commodities, diamonds and gold—because, as gradually becomes clear in the course of her book, she sees as one of the fundamental experiences underlying totalitarianism a sense of the utter expendability of people:

. . . radical evil has emerged in connection with a system in which all men have become equally superfluous. The manipulators of this system believe in their own superfluousness as much as in that of all others, and the totalitarian murderers are all the more dangerous because they do not care if they themselves are alive or dead, if they ever lived or never were born.[7]

The second strand in her account of imperialism, the seed of a new kind of community to replace the nation-state undermined by imperialist expansion, is racism. She explores the ideas of early race-theorists such as Gobineau, and emphasizes that these were quite distinct from nationalism and usually hostile to it, since their races cut across national frontiers : but she is at pains to insist that however much similarity there might be at the level of ideas between such speculation and Nazi ideology, there is a world of difference between racial theories and the reality of racist practice. Racism as an ideology strong enough to authorize genocide she traces back to the experiences of the imperialists, rootless Europeans finding themselves face to face with the tribal peoples of Africa. In a particularly vivid section,[8] drawing heavily on Conrad's story *Heart of Darkness*, she describes this encounter : the adventurers, themselves the superfluous men of Europe, who had ceased to belong to a community in which accepted conventions about what was reasonable behaviour could set limits to their impulses; and the incomprehensible life of the natives, who apparently lived as if they were part of nature instead of having superimposed upon it a human world of civilization, and who seemed all one with the incomprehensible jungle. In this situation, where the Europeans had lost their own world of the nation and the sense of reality and responsibility it engendered, while the Africans presented no alternative human world, the adventurers had a feeling of unreality and irresponsibility, the feeling, as in a dream, that everything is possible. She points to the appalling massacres of the Congo, and identifies a similar dream-like or nightmarish feeling of unreality as an essential element in totalitarianism. The racism that this situation engendered was, she thinks, of the same kind as that developed indigenously by the Boers, the European people that had lived with this con-frontation longest and reacted to it most comprehensively. She suggests that the Boers, faced in South Africa with a large black population who were uncivilized in the sense that they lived, like animals, at the mercy of nature instead of imposing a human order upon it, had developed a racist theory to protect themselves from the shattering realization that these savages were human like themselves. At the same time that they developed their ideology of superiority, however, they became like the native themselves, for instead of following the example of their European ancestors, settling a definite territory and transforming nature into their own human creation, they themselves became, like the Africans, a rootless horde of wandering people, bound together by blood, as a tribe is, and not by location, as nations are. To Hannah Arendt this rootlessness and lack of any basis for community other than blood is characteristic of race-thinking, and she finds the same negative qualities in the masses who were attracted by racist doctrines in Europe.

The third element (besides racism and the passion for expansion for its own sake) which Hannah Arendt finds in imperialism and regards as contributory to totalitarianism is 'Bureaucracy', by which she means the kind of rule developed by the imperial administrators of the British Empire. She plays on the dramatic irony that in contrast to racism, which rejected the natives as inferior and valueless beings, the ideal imperial administrator took up the white man's burden on their behalf, and yet was equally disastrous in his political effects. Bureaucracy in her sense is administrative rule, which differs from political rule in that it is irresponsible and lawless, a matter of officials taking decisions in secret and issuing decrees. Her view forms an interesting contrast to Weber's model of bureaucracy as a highly rationalized, responsible form of government that works according to rules: but the difference is partly that Weber looked at bureaucracy from the point of view of the official, from within, whereas Hannah Arendt sees it much more from the point of view of the subject. Looked at from below, the striking characteristics of this kind of rule are its mysteriousness, secrecy, unpredictability and arbitrariness—its Kafkaesque qualities. Apart from the intrinsic lawlessness of rule by decree, it was characteristic of the imperial administration that decisions were taken not only with a view to the merits of the matter in hand but in the interests of the more general process of imperial expansion, of which the administrators felt themselves to be the secret instruments. The passion for secrecy, and the sense of serving a higher purpose and being carried along by forces greater than oneself, were particularly pronounced in the imperial secret services, and Hannah Arendt draws on the writings of Lawrence of Arabia to illustrate the fascination that this combination of action with the denial of personal responsibility could have even for good men.

So far, she has been concerned with imperialist trends exemplified most clearly in the British Empire, and she has claimed that they provide the ancestry of totalitarianism in spite of the fact that it was not in Britain that totalitarianism arose but in Germany and Russia, neither of which had participated to any great extent in overseas expansion. Her case is that the trends which were apparent in overseas imperialism, and which, because of the geographical distance, could develop in the empire without destroying the institutions of the nation-state at home, were paralleled by what she calls 'Continental Imperialism' in central Europe and Russia, a much more politically dangerous phenomenon because it was on the spot. She labels as continental imperialism the pan-movements, Pan-Germanism and Pan-Slavism, and claims that like overseas imperialism they were movements for endless expansion and were hostile to the state; that the kind of so-called nationalism they propounded was not nationalism at all but akin to racism; and that they exalted power and rule by decree just as the imperial bureaucrats were doing.

It seems to her essential to distinguish between true nationalism—the attachment of a settled community, such as the French, to the land in which it has long lived, the institutions which it has developed, and the history of which it is proud—and both racism and what she calls the 'tribal nationalism' [9] of the pan-movements. By using the term 'tribal' she refers back to the way the Boers had, as she claims, become a tribe like the Africans, a horde of people linked by common blood rather than the soil in which they were rooted and the civilization and institutions they possessed. In other words, whereas a nation is held together by the concrete institutions and environment which its members share, that is to say by things outside the members, tribal nationalism defines its nation entirely in terms of supposed common blood or some metaphysical entity internal to the individual such as 'the Slav soul'. This kind of nationalism had a peculiar appeal for the mixed populations of the Austro-Hungarian monarchy, most of which had never had any institutions nor a settled location, and who were rootless as, for instance, Englishmen or Frenchmen could not be. She suggests that it had a similar appeal for the Russian intelligentsia, who were also rootless, but for different reasons, and later came to appeal to the new uprooted masses in the cities. Unlike concrete nationalism it involves no loyalty to any institutions nor restriction to any definite location, but instead is amorphous, harbouring hostility to all states and tendencies to endless expansion in order to vindicate the claim of the tribe to be the chosen people. She suggests that it is this claim to be the master-race simply by virtue of blood or inner soul that made the pan-movements especially hostile to the Jews, because in the rootless tribal existence of the Jews, their ancient claim to chosenness and their supposedly world-wide influence, the movements saw reflected what they themselves wanted. Both Pan-Germans and Pan-Slavs emphasized that they were not *parties*, which had fallen into disrepute in the half-hearted parliamentarianism of the European states, but *movements*, outside the party system altogether and proposing to replace the state rather than simply capture it. She claims that they were direct ancestors of the totalitarian movements, a claim which is straightforward enough in the case of Hitler's debt to the Pan-Germans but more startling where Stalin's debt to Pan-Slavism is concerned. She concedes that this last did not become fully apparent until the Second World War, when Stalin openly used Pan-Slav slogans in the war against Germany.

Hannah Arendt suggests that imperialism, represented in Europe by the pan-movements, was hostile to the nation-state and filled the vacuum where no basis for a real nation-state existed. She goes on to claim that loss of or absence of a nation-state was crucial in the matter of personal rights. One of the horrifying features of totalitarianism is that the victims were deprived of all those human rights that had supposedly been established as the rights of man in all civilized nations since the

French Revolution. But in fact it had become abundantly obvious before the rise of totalitarianism that these so-called human rights were utterly dependent on the existence of the concrete community of the nation-state for their enforcement, and that those who, through no fault of their own, fell outside such a community did not have them. She brings this out vividly by talking about the stateless people thrown up by the First World War and subsequent political upheavals. People who had no state, or whom their own state had denationalized, were not welcome in other states and had no legal position. Many of them found themselves herded into camps, where they were detained as if they were criminals, while those who escaped this fate were forced by their situation to transgress the law constantly, since they had no right to be in their country of refuge, nor any right to work. In either case, in spite of their innocence, they were at the mercy of the police. Hannah Arendt points out that such people were actually better off if they *did* commit a crime, say a small burglary, for that at least put them in a recognized legal position: that of the criminal, who does have certain legal rights. Even the criminal is subject to law, not merely to arbitrary power, whereas even in the democracies displaced persons were outside the law and therefore under the sole rule of police and officials, like the natives under imperialism and whole populations under totalitarianism.

We have been endeavouring to summarize the argument of Hannah Arendt's book; however, in order to convey the texture of her account we must look also at the way in which it is held together by certain notions that run like leitmotifs through the book, gathering associations as they go. While these notions are intimated in the section on antisemitism, it is in the section on imperialism that they are developed, and then used in the section on totalitarianism itself. The central notion is perhaps the notion of superfluousness, and this is surrounded by a cluster of connected negative concepts, rootlessness, statelessness, homelessness, selflessness, loneliness. The notion of superfluousness is first fully developed, as we have seen, with reference to the imperialist adventurers in Africa and the Conradian picture of hollow, shadowy men, escaped from the reality of civilization, confronted by the apparent unreality of native life which seemed to present them with infinite possibilities. The superfluousness of the adventurers is connected with the rootlessness of the Boers, who had, like the natives they confronted, become tribal and defined themselves not in terms of any concrete human world but only in terms of their abstract inner quality of race. Again, rootlessness was the condition of the East European peoples among whom nationalism was 'tribal' because it was abstract, with no concrete achievements to refer to, only supposed inner qualities. Rootlessness here merges into statelessness, the condition of many displaced persons after the First World War, which made it obvious that those outside a concrete human community have no rights and have indeed become superfluous. Again, the condition of these displaced people prefigures for Hannah Arendt the experience of masses uprooted by social and economic changes, who, having no community to guarantee their worth to themselves, could feel not only superfluous but selfless, and give total commitment to movements. Being homeless in the world, they had no basis for common sense, no community to assure them as to what was real and what not; and in their loneliness they could only turn to the reassurance of a consistent fiction.

In Hannah Arendt's book, the helplessness of the mass of the uprooted, homeless and lonely is contrasted dialectically with the sense of omnipotence of those no less superfluous men who believe that they are the vehicle of superhuman forces. She finds in imperialism the notion of indefinite expansion as a pseudo-natural process, halted by no demand for stability, and in the imperial bureaucrats and secret agents men who felt themselves to be merely the instruments of this expansive force. This is linked with the experience of superfluousness, in that the men escaping from Europe slipped gladly into a selfless playing of the game of imperialist adventure for its own sake. The same exhilaration at submerging oneself in the advance of forces greater than oneself recurs in the Pan-Slav exaltation of power as a divine force, and in the deification of nature and history in totalitarian ideology so that, according to Hannah Arendt, even the totalitarian rulers felt themselves to be only instruments in the execution of natural or historical laws. In the concentration camps, helplessness and omnipotence meet: here was the proof both that everything is possible and that all men are superfluous. Total domination, indeed, *makes* men superfluous by depriving them of their rights, their individuality, their existence in the memory of others, and even the possibility of rebelling against their fate.

CRITICAL REMARKS

In attempting to summarize the main lines of Hannah Arendt's account of totalitarianism and its origins we have so far refrained from criticism. However, it must be obvious that a great many objections can be raised against it, and some of these we propose to discuss briefly now.

First of all, and perhaps most basically, we can quarrel with the very substance of her analysis, with her model of totalitarianism itself, and particularly with the way she conflates Nazism and Stalinism to produce it. Her position here is somewhat ambiguous. On the one hand, the book is unquestionably dominated by Nazism. This point can be most simply made by pointing out that whereas the evolution of racism in general and antisemitism in particular, the Nazi ideology, is a central theme of the book, Marxism-Leninism is never discussed at all, and of the specific content of Stalinist ideology she has very little to say. Again, whereas a quasi-causal link between imperialism and Nazism is plausibly made through Pan-Germanism, of which Nazism was clearly a descendant, in the case of Stalinism Hannah Arendt has to claim a much more dubious ancestry by way of Pan-Slavism, the connection of which with Stalinism is scarcely obvious. In some ways, therefore, the book gives the impression of being conceived around Nazism, and having had Stalinism added on, perhaps because at the time of writing Nazism was defunct but Stalinism was still a living menace.

However, the notion that her concern with Stalinism is something of an aside, while plausible when one is reading the first two sections of the book, must be given up as soon as one comes to her model of totalitarianism itself, for this is clearly a conflation of both Nazism and Stalinism. In describing the features of totalitarianism she draws examples and illustrations from both regimes indiscriminately, and the full model exhibits features that were never fully realized in either country singly: for instance, it includes both the refinements of total domination in the Nazi concentration camps and the show trials and false confessions of Stalinist party members. That is to say, Hannah Arendt is not simply writing about Nazism and finding Stalinism sufficiently similar in certain features to be relevant. On the contrary, what she is analysing is *totalitarianism* conceived as a thing in itself, a concrete universal with a form and logic of its own, of which so far, as it happens, only two manifestations have appeared. This is an important point which we should perhaps emphasize: totalitarianism as Hannah Arendt conceives of it is not simply a convenient label for bringing out the resemblances between two discrete sets of happenings: it is a whole, a system, the parts of which hang together, and which manifested itself in two places at the same time because very broad trends within modern civilization gave rise to it. This systematic character of her model comes out when, as frequently happens, she explains events and developments in Germany and Russia by referring to the inner logic of totalitarianism, which had to develop in certain ways. For instance [10] she explains the duplication of offices in Nazi Germany by referring to the essential instability of totalitarianism:

. . . since knowledge of whom to obey and a comparatively permanent settlement of hierarchy would introduce an element of stability which is essentially absent from totalitarian rule, the Nazis constantly disavowed real authority whenever it had come into the open and created new instances of government compared with which the former became a shadow government.

Again, she emphasizes that totalitarianism is an affair of masses: in Germany Nazism was from the first a mass organization whereas, she says,[11] Stalin 'had . . . to create' a mass society in order to bring about totalitarianism. This suggests either that Stalin was deliberately setting out to create totalitarianism, having in mind a system clearly envisaged; or else perhaps that totalitarianism was the doom of our times and Stalin was, in the Hegelian manner, fulfilling his historic role in bringing it about. In either case there is no room left for contingency in its development. Also, she talks about totalitarianism [12] in terms that make one forget that, by her own account, there have so far only been two cases of it—evidently

39

feeling that these are significant rather as instances of a general phenomenon than simply in themselves.

Thus although her book might seem in some respects like a book about Nazism plus an analogy with Stalinism, her equation of the two is actually crucial to her claim that it is necessary to recognize a special thing, totalitarianism, that is manifest in our time and must be explained by the general trends of our time. Clearly, if it is agreed that Nazism and Stalinism are properly described as cases of this same phenomenon, then an explanation that will cover both must be of a general nature, not, for instance, confined to details of the particular political and economic situation and cultural heritage of Germany and Russia. This is bound up with another point that we shall have to go into later, the question of what precisely it is that needs to be explained. Hannah Arendt insists that totalitarianism as a system was deliberately constructed by its perpetrators, thereby excluding any understanding of it as the outcome of contingent events and actions. She claims, for example, that the concentration camps were *experiments* in total domination, and says in fact [13] that the reason we need to try to understand them is not the suffering, which has always been present in human life, but the radical attempt to change human nature. Clearly, if it is once admitted that Nazism and Stalinism represent the same phenomenon, it does then seem plausible to assume that both systems were designed (whether at the level of deliberate intention or through the 'cunning of reason') rather than contingent.

It is therefore rather a crucial part of her argument to claim that Nazism and Stalinism are examples of the same phenomenon. However, is this claim justified, and is it really helpful to talk about totalitarianism as a system in the way that she does? It is certainly true enough that both Nazism and Stalinism were guilty of appalling crimes on a massive scale. However, Hannah Arendt herself points out [14] that the deliberate degradation and extermination of the Nazi camps, in which she sees the nub of totalitarianism, was absent from the Russian camps, where death and suffering were more a matter of neglect than of policy. In other words it is by her own account arguable that whereas Nazism produced something new in the history of human suffering, Stalin's camps represented an extension on a vast scale of the traditional methods of Tsarist despotism. Again it is certainly true that in Russia, as well as in Germany, there was a leader, a mass party and an ideology dominating the whole of life; but here again, by Hannah Arendt's own account, these are not enough to constitute totalitarianism. These features still exist in Russia, but she has subsequently agreed that since Stalin's death Russia has ceased to be totalitarian. For a totalitarian state in her sense is not simply an ideologically dominated police state, but something much more radical. To be in accord with her model it must lack the stability of ordinary despotism, and be in constant motion, internally through purges, and externally in aiming at world domination, thereby making ordinary power-politics impossible. She says herself [15] that Russia since Stalin's death has not been totalitarian in this sense, having developed both considerable internal stability and a comparatively conventional and comprehensible foreign policy.

At the time when *The Origins of Totalitarianism* was written, Stalin was still alive and the future looked very black. In her prefaces and additions to subsequent editions Hannah Arendt has noted that Russia has ceased to be totalitarian in her sense, without perhaps realizing how much this admission weakens her model: for if totalitarianism were the systematic whole that she suggests, and were as she claims the outcome of the most general of our century's trends, it would surely take more than the death of one particular leader to stop it. In the first edition of the book, evidently thinking of the end of Nazism, she remarked [16] that totalitarianism might well be short lived because it aimed at world domination, and therefore necessarily raised up enemies whom it could not even play off against one another in the conventional manner of power politics. She said then that it was nevertheless vital to understand totalitarianism because it pointed to the problems of our time—the senselessness of life, the experience of superfluousness, the loss of morality. However, if this is so it seems extraordinary both that totalitarianism has not arisen in more places, and that it could cease in Russia—not even, as in Germany, as a result of destruction from outside, but apparently in the manner of old-style despotism where the personality of the particular despot is all-important.

For these reasons, one may doubt whether her model can really be extended beyond Nazism, her starting point. However, if Nazism is to be considered as a case on its own, not as an example of a more general phenomenon, one may question whether it is plausible to interpret it as such a purposive system; and furthermore, if it is Nazism, not any more general phenomenon, that needs to be explained, then the explanation should surely be less general and wide-ranging than that Hannah Arendt offers, more specifically related to the question why this happened in Germany and not elsewhere.

Having expressed doubts about what Hannah Arendt is trying to describe and explain, we shall go on to raise more doubts about the explanation she offers. This can be queried at various levels. To take what is perhaps the most basic level first, it is by no means clear what exactly she means by many of the most important terms that she uses in her explanation, notably, for instance, 'nation-state', 'Bourgeoisie' and 'masses'. As we have pointed out in summarizing her argument, her conception of the nation-state plays a crucial role in her account of the origins of totalitarianism, for she sees both antisemitism and more especially imperialism as forces which were hostile to the nation-state and which in destroying it destroyed also the old basis for community and rights. It is clear that her basic paradigm of the nation-state is post-revolutionary France; what is by no means clear, however, is what other states would count as nation-states in her sense. She writes about the downfall of the nation-state in terms that might give one the impression that Europe had consisted of such states until the coming of imperialism. When one considers, however, that most of Europe, and particularly the German and Austro-Hungarian parts of it with which she is most concerned, had belonged to states that could not possibly be thought of as national, it is difficult to see what she can be talking about. Again, she maintains that imperialism was a force destructive of the nation-state. But what nation-states were in fact destroyed by imperialism? Most of her imperialist examples are taken from the British Empire, and Britain did not disintegrate under the stress of imperialism, nor show the slightest tendency to become totalitarian. The states within which her totalitarian movements grew up were quite the reverse of national, and while it may well be the case that both their adherents and their victims were rootless people who had lost a community, it was hardly a *national* community that they had lost. This is one of the many cases in the book where it is impossible to pin down for consideration precisely what she means because she talks in generalized terms without making clear their relation to specific, concrete occurrences. She talks of the nation-state without saying which states she means; of 'the bourgeoisie' as the begetters of imperialism without further specification; of 'the masses' who replaced previous classes in society without any indication of who might or might not qualify for this category or what grounds she has for claiming that such people were the mainstay of Nazism. Her whole technique is in fact a social scientist's nightmare. Open to criticism at the same level is her habit of asserting startling opinions without giving any evidence for them; her reliance on literary evidence, for instance her use of Conrad's *Heart of Darkness* as evidence of the nature of imperialism; and her habit of playing with images to induce conviction in her readers.[17] We have not sufficient space to discuss the various instances of this type of vagueness, nor the defences that might be made of them; we wish merely to draw attention to a general lack of precise reference to concrete things in her use of terms and manner of arguing.

Her explanation can, then, be attacked in detail at many points. At a more general level, it may be doubted whether the trends she discusses do in fact explain totalitarianism. It may be the case, for instance, that administrative rule in British India or racism in South Africa had points in common with police rule and the extermination of the Jews under Nazism: but is there any causal connection from the one to the other? If totalitarianism had arisen in Britain it would undoubtedly be to the point to uncover aspects of British imperialism like the development of bureaucratic rule, the passion of the administrators for secrecy and the intoxication of agents like Lawrence at finding themselves the tools of forces greater than themselves: but does this really help to explain what happened in Germany or Russia? Where is the connecting link? Hannah Arendt tries to supply it by labelling the pan-movements 'Continental' imperialism and suggesting that the same forces were at work there in Europe as overseas in the British Empire. However, this merely begs the question by assuming mysterious forces working in the background and driving both Britons and East Europeans in the same direction. In any case, given the tradition of bureaucracy and despotism in both Austria-Hungary and Russia it is hardly necessary to look to esoteric parallels in the British Empire to find explanations for such tendencies in the pan-movements.

One can appreciate that the question of causation presented a difficult problem for Hannah Arendt precisely because of her methodological sophistication. On the one hand she wanted to explain totalitarianism in the sense of making intelligible how it could have come about, and that involved finding causes adequate to the result; on the other hand, the last thing she wished to do was to produce a chain of causes that would seem to show that totalitarianism was inevitable, and to deny power to choose and to act just as much as the totalitarian ideologies themselves had done. She states [18] in replying to a review of her book by Eric Voegelin that her object was to analyse the chief elements that 'crystallized' into totalitarianism—elements that were presumably present in European culture. This seems to leave the question of causation open, although it does not really explain what the relation is between, say, Lawrence of Arabia and Hitler. It may be doubted, therefore, what power her explanation actually has to explain totalitarianism. One of the problems is that, if totalitarianism is conceived of as a systematic entity, a political phenomenon of our century, separable in principle from the two supposed cases of its occurrence, then any explanation of it must be of a very general kind, referring not merely to particular German and Russian history but to European civilization in general. General explanations of this kind have the disadvantage that their number is limited only by human ingenuity, and it is hard to see what kind of reason could be given for validating one and invalidating others. It is interesting to compare Hannah Arendt's understanding of totalitarianism with that of Eric Voegelin, who resembles her in being an extraordinarily able political theorist whose culture is also German and whose manner of thought is equally hostile to American political science. According to Voegelin [19] totalitarianism should be understood as the culmination of a Christian heresy, of which liberalism, Marxism, Nazism and virtually all modern political doctrines are variants. This heresy he calls 'Gnosticism', and it consists, baldly, in the attempt to establish secularized versions of the Kingdom of God on earth. Voegelin's explanation is worked out in much less detail than Hannah Arendt's, but it is on an equally grand scale, and is equally impossible to validate.

Given the problems of ever validating an explanation sufficiently general to account for what is supposed to be a general phenomenon, it may be pertinent to ask whether perhaps it is misguided to look for such an explanation in the first place. We have already suggested that Hannah Arendt's conception of totalitarianism as a systematic entity, resting as it appears to do on the equation of Stalin's Russia and Hitler's Germany, may be questioned. If in fact 'totalitarianism' as a general phenomenon is really an intellectual construct invented to cover a combination of aspects of two rather different systems, then the problem of explanation is rather that of explaining the occurrence of Nazism on the one hand and Stalinism on the other. And although Hannah Arendt does concentrate mainly on trying to provide an explanation of Nazism, we may question whether so elaborate an explanation is really necessary. As we have seen, she believes that totalitarianism is a systematic thing which develops according to its own logic, and that totalitarianism in Germany and Russia was deliberately planned, constructed purposely. The latter point comes out particularly in her account of the concentration camps, which she regards as deliberate experiments in total domination. Consequently, even if she were not committed to regarding Nazism and Stalinism as equivalent, she would still feel it necessary to explain Nazism as a deliberate construction, and to explain this must involve fairly general considerations.

However, are there really grounds for supposing that Nazism *was* purposive to that extent? If it were a system deliberately conceived, propagandized and constructed then certainly the question of how this could be so seems to demand an explanation in terms of German civilization, if not in terms of European culture in general. But what of the possibility that it was all less purposive and more contingent than Hannah Arendt seems to allow? Suppose that the system was not in fact con-

45

ceived as a whole by anyone, but brought about as a result of a great many events and actions, contributed to by many men none of whom fully realized what he was doing? In that case the kind of explanation that would be appropriate would be in terms firstly of the eternal human capacity for cruelty, sufficiently manifested in recorded history; secondly of the characteristics of modern life, such as rapid communications and bureaucratic efficiency, that enable the characters and decisions of a few men to affect millions; and thirdly of the specific web and sequence of contingent events and actions whereby the Nazis rose to power in Germany and gradually moved to more and more radical activities. The possibility that it could have taken place like this without anyone fully realizing or intending what was happening, is, ironically, brought out by Hannah Arendt's own study of Adolf Eichmann, written at the time of his trial and execution. She subtitles the book 'The Banality of Evil' to underline her central point, namely the utter disproportion between the crimes Eichmann had participated in and his own consciousness of what he was doing. She emphasizes the perplexity of the judges, faced with such enormous crimes and such a pigmy criminal. If it should be the case that many of those involved participated in Nazism in this dream-like way, never quite realizing the significance of what they were doing, then the central problem of Hannah Arendt's book on totalitarianism ceases to be a problem. Her book is written to answer the assumed question, how could people *mean to do* these things and carry them out? But if there is no deliberate intention, no full consciousness to be found, if it is all a fabric of contingency, then only contingent explanations are appropriate.

Ironically it may be the case that Hannah Arendt's account of the origins of totalitarianism is open to precisely the same objections that she raises against totalitarian ideologies. She notes that the charm of ideology for men whose world has become incomprehensible is that it provides a consistent framework into which everything appears to fit; it uncovers the hidden mechanics of events, explains all accidents by reference to forces working behind the scenes, but is destructive of common sense and reality precisely because it leaves no room for contingency—it is more consistent than real life ever is.

. . . totalitarian movements conjure up a lying world of consistency which is more adequate to the needs of the human mind than reality itself; in which, through sheer imagination, uprooted masses can feel at home and are spared the never-ending shocks which real life and real experiences deal to human beings and their expectations.[20]

Such is the charm of consistency that where facts do appear to contradict it, the adherent of an ideology will prefer the system to the facts. Is it not the case that Hannah Arendt herself tries to provide an account of the incomprehensible happenings of her time which also depends on uncovering hidden forces, and which shares with ideological explanations the tendency to make everything fit and, in cases of conflict, to prefer consistency to contingent fact?

We have raised (though not discussed in full)[21] so many objections to Hannah Arendt's book that the reader may by this time be asking whether this enterprise is not self-destructive: if it is indeed possible to quarrel with her thesis on so many grounds, is it worth reading, much less worth writing about? And this brings us to the curious but undeniable point that even if all these objections hold, her book would still be extremely illuminating, and more so than many to which fewer objections can be made. Why is this? How is it that even if we deny most of the theses that a book contains we can still insist that it is a remarkably good book? Answering this question will give us some indication of the qualities that make Hannah Arendt's work stand out among political and philosophical writings of the present day.

First of all, her book is worth reading because it is a very considerable work of art. In it she has woven many diverse themes together into an intricate and enthralling pattern, combining a remarkable density of ideas with great subtlety of organization. Her writing matches the brilliance of her ideas, and makes the book vivid and enthralling. There can be few political works that are hard to put down, but this is one of them. Her imagination and the vividness of her writing are particularly striking when she is writing about Nazism, for more conventional political scientists' accounts of such phenomena as concentration camps are inclined—by their very academicism and detachment—to miss the point and convey nothing of the things they seek to describe. Further-

more, whether or not one accepts Hannah Arendt's account
of totalitarianism and its origins, one has to admit that it is an
intensely reflective book, so that even when it fails as history it
succeeds as reflection.

If it seems paradoxical to say that reflections of permanent
value may be based on dubious history, only consider the case
of Burke's *Reflections on the Revolution in France*. To accept his
account of the events in France and the reasons for them would
be unwise, and yet the ideas to which his reflections on those
events and supposed causes gave rise have illuminated political
thinking ever since. Similarly, the interest of *The Origins of
Totalitarianism* is that it is a highly theoretical book: in contemplating the events of her time, in seeking for their causes and in
identifying antecedents as significant, Hannah Arendt is all
the time rising from particular facts to exploratory reflections
of a general nature, in the course of which she arrives at conceptions and ways of seeing things that are generally illuminating and that she has since followed up and elaborated into a
more extensive political theory. We shall be looking at this
political theory in the later chapters of this book; let us look
now at the way in which some of its key notions and emphases
can be seen emerging out of her reflections on totalitarianism.

One set of connected conceptions leads to the notion which
(as we shall see in Chapter 4) she later developed of 'the
World'. In *The Origins of Totalitarianism* we see her reflecting
upon racism and the experiences which gave rise to it, and
thinking about its autonomous development among the Boers
in South Africa. Imagining their situation vis-à-vis the natives,
it strikes her that besides their appearance and their language
the Africans were different from civilized men in that they
were closer to nature, they lived on nature instead of having
transformed it by their own activities as, for instance, the
Dutch in Holland so conspicuously had. They were strange
because they were *natural*, and to that extent non-human. She
begins to build up an antithesis between nature and the
human world, seeing what is human as a very *un*natural thing,
carefully constructed and always liable to disintegrate. So far
in this example the notion is (in Oakeshott's term) only
'intimated'. A further intimation comes in her chapter on 'The
Decline of the Nation-State and the End of the Rights of Man',

when she is discussing the appalling situation of displaced persons after the First World War who found that, having no state to claim them and give them a legal position, they had no rights at all simply in virtue of their humanity. Mere human *nature* gave them no claims: only the artificial human world could do that and once they were thrust outside it they were in a 'state of nature' and apparently superfluous. Further connected reflections come in her discussion of ideology, when she is suggesting that super-logical systems of thought, however fictitious, may appeal to the masses of our century because they are lonely, cut off from their fellows. She suggests that such consistent fictions can be criticized only by common sense, and common sense requires a settled community of people to establish it and confirm one another's judgments. Again, a non-natural and destructible human artifice is necessary to underpin one of the most basic human attributes.

As we shall see, the whole notion of 'the World' and the worldlessness of modern times became one of Hannah Arendt's most illuminating conceptions; in *The Origins of Totalitarianism*, however, one can see her engaged in the process of thinking that led to it, reflecting on one set of events and forming a conception which becomes clarified by further reflections on another. Again, we shall see as we proceed with this investigation of her thought that her chief preoccupation in political theory is freedom, and that her understanding of freedom is unusual. In *The Origins of Totalitarianism*, however, one can see the reflections against which her conception of freedom is asserted and by reference to which it must be understood. For instance, in the course of a sensitive and fascinating exploration of the situation of secularized Jews in nineteenth-century society [22] she talks of how these Jews came to define themselves in a new way, not as members of a community and a faith but as embodiments of *Jewishness*, a supposedly internal racial characteristic. In other words what they did and said was expected by themselves and others to manifest not them as persons but their Jewishness. There is an echo of this experience in her study of Lawrence of Arabia, whom she describes as exhilarated by the submergence of his personality in his work as a secret agent, the feeling that great forces were working through him. Again, this connects in her mind with the determinism of the ideologies, their assumption that individual human action is insignificant, and with the deliberate destruction of personality in the concentration camps; and there is intimated in her reflections the conception of freedom she later elaborated and asserted against these trends of the times, the conception of freedom as the spontaneous, unpredictable action and speech among themselves of irreplaceable individuals.

We have looked very briefly at two of the centres of reflection in her book, two conceptions which have become particularly prominent in her subsequent writings; however, the reader will find interesting general reflections throughout, and for the sake of these and the process of thought they punctuate, her book must have value whether or not one is prepared to accept its main theses. It is as a thinker rather than as an historian that Hannah Arendt has a claim to fame. In the following chapters we shall explore her thought, partly intimated in *The Origins of Totalitarianism*, and developed most fully in *The Human Condition*.

3

The Human Condition

Man, this flexible being, who submits himself in society to the thoughts and impressions of his fellow-men, is equally capable of knowing his own nature when it is shown to him as it is and of losing it to the point where he has no realisation that he is robbed of it. (Montesquieu, quoted by Hannah Arendt [1])

It has often been pointed out that the different political theories can be regarded as the working out of different understandings of human nature and the human condition. The medieval philosophers' Rational Animal set on earth to serve God obviously requires a different political structure from Hobbes's mutually hostile, desire-driven automatons or Locke's industrious, peaceable men of property. However, these different points of view should not be seen as being based upon entirely different observations, as though the men Thomas Aquinas was acquainted with were altogether different from those Thomas Hobbes saw around him. Still less should they be regarded as arbitrary opinions, with the implication that since no objective human nature exists everyone is entitled to his own view of these matters. Rather should they be seen as caricatures, selective observations designed to draw attention to aspects of man's nature and condition that the philosopher considers particularly significant or particularly neglected in his time. When, for instance, Marx characterized man as essentially the Worker, he was not ignorant of nor did he wish to deny other human capacities; rather, he wished to draw attention to an aspect of the human condition that seemed to him at once immensely important and grossly neglected. Any account of human nature is at the same time an exercise in observation and description and a judgment of what is most significant, and the latter aspect commonly predominates over the former.

Like other political theories, Hannah Arendt's is rooted in and constantly refers to her understanding of the human condition, which she has articulated most fully in her book of that title. Like other accounts, it is prescriptive, incorporating judgments as to what human capacities are particularly significant and most fully human, and it is perhaps as startlingly unconventional an account from the standpoint of twentieth-century orthodoxies as Hobbes's was from the point of view of early seventeenth-century conventions. It may seem at first sight a paradoxical enterprise to propose to us a view of the human condition that contradicts so many of our ordinary assumptions: do we not all know from personal experience what this condition is? This is not a question that she discusses explicitly, and our account of her method must be to some extent conjectural, but it seems clear that her answer would take two parts.

In the first place, all men have a double identity. Each is both one particular individual—who is never an exact replica of anyone else, and who is always capable of thinking and acting in new ways—and at the same time also a member of the human race, plunged into the same world; confronted by the same fate and sharing the same capacities for experience as other men. Because of his individuality, he can make discoveries and have something to communicate to other men; but because of his membership in the human species he is *able* to communicate with them, and to draw with them upon the reservoir of human experience which so many generations have accumulated. All men share in the same human condition in that there are certain experiences, such as hunger, thirst and confrontation with death, which none of them can escape; but they also share in a host of possible experiences which many of them may never actually have, and of which they may even remain quite ignorant. Any particular man or group of men may therefore be quite unaware of large aspects of human experience upon which they have never happened to stumble, although these are possibilities for them also. They may therefore give a distorted account of the human condition, even if they are able to describe faithfully those experiences they actually know at first hand.

More important, however, as a source of distortion in such

accounts is a second point, namely that explicitly articulated doctrines, because of their caricature-like quality, very often fail to do justice to the experience even of those who formulate or accept them, although until another articulation that is more faithful to experience is presented to them the people concerned do not realize that anything is wrong. Consider, for example, the impact of Burke's romanticism upon such men as James Mackintosh, author of the *Vindiciae Gallicae*, who had previously thought about politics in terms of eighteenth-century rationalist and utilitarian conventions. They had of course always known such things as that old ways of doing things attract strong emotional ties; that people tend to accept without question what has always been so but to look with suspicion on new things; that kings and nobles have a glamour that commoners do not; that schemes which seem excellent in theory can come adrift in practice—and so on. However, they had accepted doctrines that took no account of these things and of much else that they knew, and did not notice the gap between doctrine and ordinary experience until it was articulated by Burke and underlined by the course of the French Revolution. It is all too common for men to believe earnestly in doctrines which almost all their everyday experience contradicts.

Hannah Arendt's task in giving her account of the human condition, then, is twofold. It is partly to correct existing doctrines by providing an articulate theory more faithful to the experience they ignore, in the hope that, provided with this articulation, her readers will recognize their own experience in it; and partly, by making use of the experience of other ages, to draw our attention to possibilities that we had never realized were open to us. In both these tasks she draws constantly upon our language as a repository of experience. The languages that we speak cover a far wider range of possible experiences than the theories that we subscribe to, not least because they preserve the memory of experiences that were named and talked about in the past. As long as we do not entirely replace these inherited languages by custom-built jargon (a fate that she fears for social scientists) we have a refuge on our own doorsteps from the narrowness of our theories. Furthermore, the languages of former cultures, like those of the Greeks and the Romans, remain repositories of their experiences, and can reveal to us human possibilities that our own language has ceased to chronicle. Accordingly, as we shall see, in her effort to provide us with a more adequate description of our human condition, she constantly refers to the ancient languages, or develops commonly unnoticed distinctions within our own.

In *The Human Condition* she is concerned with the various modes of human *activity* and their respective dignity: she is explicitly not concerned with trying to judge the relative merits of activity and thought. She is herself of course a thinker, and she constantly makes clear in her writings that she regards thinking, the attempt to gain an understanding of our situation and activities, as no mere intellectual amusement but a task of great value. She has nothing in common with Marx's turning of philosophy against itself and use of it to exalt activity over thought. However, her claim is that because the tradition of Western culture is so much a philosopher's tradition, in which the philosophic evaluation of thought over activity was only reinforced by the Christian ideal of contemplation, human activity has not been sufficiently thought about and its modes not clearly articulated, even by those, like Marx, who tried to turn the tradition upside-down. Her aim, then, is to leave aside the realm of thought and contemplation without attempting to compare its dignity with that of action, and to describe and relate to one another the various forms of human activity. In doing so she is of course drawing upon and referring to constant human experience, available in principle to men everywhere; but in making her distinctions and her judgments, and especially in characterizing 'Action', she refers particularly to the experience of the Greeks, who lived and talked about their experience before Socrates and his disciples had created the philosophic tradition and led the attention of subsequent generations away from activity to thought. The modes that she distinguishes as basic components of human activity are three: Labour, Work and Action. We shall look briefly at each of these in turn, and then consider in more detail her reflections upon them.

LABOUR

One obvious class of human activities, and one which is hardly likely to be forgotten since Marx laid so much stress upon it, is that range of activities which man cannot avoid if he is to stay alive and to perpetuate his species. Crudely, man must eat before he can do anything else. Nor is this something that can be accomplished once for all—he must go on finding and producing more food to enable him to eat every day of his life. There is of course nothing specifically human about this situation. All animals spend virtually their entire lives serving the process of life itself, seeking food, devouring it, pro-creating successors and feeding them. Animals live under the dominion of biological necessity, and so, as far as their lives also are a matter of production and consumption, do men. This is most obvious in the case of those human beings who live nearest to nature, and least in a human world of their own construction: hunters and food-gatherers, who must spend almost all their time and energy simply keeping themselves alive. This basic activity, shared with animals and dictated by biological necessity, is what Hannah Arendt calls labour. Less primitive men have managed to emancipate themselves from natural necessity in some degree, in recent times by building machines to do more and more of this labour for them; in earlier civilizations, liberation from the constant grinding pressure of nature's necessity could be achieved by the fortunate few only by redoubling the weight of necessity upon the less fortunate—that is to say, by enslaving them in order to make them serve the biological needs of their masters as well as themselves.

Characteristic of labour is its combination of necessity with futility. It can be interrupted only at the cost of life, and yet its products are consumed as soon as they are produced, leaving nothing permanent to show for the human effort that has gone into them. Even the pleasures of consumption are transient things, constantly lost and constantly needing to be repeated. From the toil and pain that go into it, nothing emerges from labour but the perpetuation of life in an endlessly repetitive cycle. It seems significant to Hannah Arendt that the activity of giving birth, of painfully reproducing the species, should be described in so many languages by the same word as the toil that maintains life.

WORK

Contrasted with Labour, which consists in the endless, repetitive, inescapable service of biological necessity, work is *unnatural*, for it consists in working upon and transforming given nature, wrenching substances from their natural context and using them as material for the multitudinous man-made things with which civilized man surrounds himself to make a human world—a world characteristically his own and able to survive the swings of the biological cycle. When the archaeologist excavates the cities of forgotten peoples, he knows of course that they, like all other men, must have spent much of their time and energy labouring to keep themselves alive. But as labourers and consumers they remain anonymous: they are given an identity, characterized as possessors of a civilization, by their artifacts, the durable products of work, the buildings, tools, vessels and monuments which formed their human world and survived their biological life. There may be parallels with work in the activities of bees, ants and beavers, but labour is common to *all* species: work, the production of things for use rather than consumption, is characteristically human as labour is not. The products of work are of course not infinitely durable —they wear out in the course of use. But they are not designed for consumption as are the products of labour, and they are not futile or repetitive. They are the creations of man, and once created they stand over against him, forming his specifically human, unnatural world. For this reason, work has sometimes been regarded as the defining characteristic of man, who is *Homo faber*. It is as creator of objects that man asserts himself as lord of creation, for his activity involves dominating and destroying what is there naturally, killing the tree, for example, and using its wood as material in order to impose upon it his own form and conception. The worker, unlike the labourer, does not merely follow the dictates of a natural need: he forms a project and carries it through, adjusting his means to the end he aims at. His activity is not an endless cycle, it has a definite beginning and consummation.

In the modern age, the direction of craftsmen's ingenuity

towards the making of machines for use in the process of production has brought the skill of the worker to the aid of the labourer, easing his toil and increasing his productivity. According to Hannah Arendt, however,[2] it has not fundamentally changed the condition of labouring as an endless, repetitive cycle in which the labourer is at the mercy of the rhythm of processes outside himself, whether natural or man-created. Labourers have become the servants of machines instead of servants of nature; their activity is less back-breaking as a result, but it nevertheless remains an unfree and futile activity, producing goods for consumption in a process precisely as repetitive and determined as the life-process itself. This differs from the activity of the craftsman engaged in work, whose struggle to impose form upon nature is a vindication of his freedom, and who sees his justification in the object that he makes. Hannah Arendt maintains that the result of the development of machines has been to turn more and more craftsmen into labourers, and more and more objects into articles of consumption, thereby reducing the permanence and durability of the world by which we are surrounded until it no longer provides a lasting home for human beings.[3]

One of the characteristics of work as opposed to labour (and, as we shall see, to action) is that it is according to Hannah Arendt an inherently solitary activity. Craftsmanship, the making of a durable thing that will form part of the human world, is not something that can be improved by teamwork: where, as in modern industry, the various component activities of making a thing are broken up and performed successively by different men this ceases to be work and becomes labour, the serving of an automatic process, which an indefinite number of men can engage in simultaneously. In the modern world, according to Hannah Arendt, almost the only remaining domain of work as opposed to labour is the creation of works of art.

ACTION

Labour is the activity to which men are doomed by biological necessity, by the need to stay alive: man as labourer is a producer and consumer. Work is the condition of civilized existence, the domination of nature in order to create accord-

57

ing to human design a world over against nature in which humans can live and be at home. Action, the third and highest of Hannah Arendt's categories of human activity, is harder to describe. The kind of activities the term is likely to suggest to the modern reader are those of the 'man of action', the seeker of adventure, who probably engages in violence. Again, since Marx, with his exhortations to men to stop merely thinking and act, the term has overtones of violent revolution. It is therefore necessary to make clear that although, as we shall see, Hannah Arendt also thinks of revolutionary situations as one of the pre-eminent fields of action, and although her use of the term also has overtones of adventure, nevertheless action in her sense is not equivalent to violence, and is indeed dissociated from it. The men of revolutions engage in action in her sense not primarily by building barricades and shooting down soldiers but by stepping forward from their private lives into the light of public affairs, by taking the initiative and starting things, by embarking upon common enterprises and experiencing the exhilaration of freedom. Action may incidentally involve violence, particularly in situations of war or revolution, but it is not the violence that makes it action.

In writing about action Hannah Arendt is engaged in the creation of a new category by means of phenomenological description, of isolating from the mass of human experience certain aspects of life to which we do not ordinarily pay specific attention and bringing them into prominence. Her previous categories of labour and work, while significant in themselves, are there chiefly to help to define action and mark out its place within human activity; for it is her understanding of action and all that it implies that lies at the very centre of her thought. In creating this category and giving it such a central place she is endeavouring to vindicate human freedom —the fact that every human being represents a new beginning in the world, and has the capacity to change things, to start something new, to do or say something that could not have been foreseen or expected. Throughout her descriptions of action there is an implied contrast with the sociological categories that are so influential nowadays, categories such as 'behaviour', 'role-playing', 'doing a job', 'belonging to a class', etc. What all of these have in common is that men seen in terms of them are interchangeable for one another, whereas what Hannah Arendt is concerned to stress is, as she puts it, the fact of 'Natality': the fact that we are not only all mortal, doomed to extinction,[4] but that each of us represents something new and unique in the world and is capable of doing the unexpected and acting in ways that no role-prescriptions can foresee.

Action is the category of activities that are in no sense dictated by the demands of nature, nor consist in the solitary creation of things to be added to the human artifice, but which are carried on among men in the public world which they constitute among themselves. They are made possible by what Hannah Arendt calls the human condition of 'Plurality'. By this she means that all human beings are of the same species, and are sufficiently alike to understand one another, but yet no two men are ever interchangeable as individuals, nor are the points of view from which they see the common world ever the same. Each is capable of acting in relation to his fellows in ways that are individual and original, and in doing so of contributing to a network of actions and relationships that is infinitely complex and unpredictable, just as a conversation is unpredictable compared with a piece of deductive reasoning. This web of deeds and relationships is the outcome of action, and it is in action (and in speech, which Hannah Arendt commonly couples with it, following the example of the Greeks, whose hero Achilles was a 'doer of great deeds and speaker of great words') that people reveal themselves as the unique individuals they are. In labour the individuality of men is submerged in their common service to natural necessity—here, indeed, men do as the social scientists say they do, they 'behave', 'play roles' and 'belong to classes'. In work there is more scope for individuality, in that each work of art or craftsmanship carries an individual signature in its style; but the creator is still subordinate to the end-product, which survives him but tells us nothing about him except that he was capable of creating it. It is only in action, in initiating undertakings and interacting with one another, that men, these unique individuals, reveal what they personally are. Even they themselves learn this only from the event, and cannot know in advance what kind of self they will reveal in their actions, any more than they can know where their actions will lead. Labour is predictable because it is bound by necessity; work contains an element of freedom but once the process of making an object is embarked upon the activity is bound by the end at which it aims; action alone is free, for it consists above all in the capacity to initiate, to alter situations by engaging in them, to perform continual miracles of unpredictability that can be put together to make an intelligible story only after the event. However, while action is free to start processes and bring about events, it is outside the power of the actor to control the consequences of what he does. Each action of his sets off processes and enters into the inextricable web of actions and events to which all other participators in the common world also contribute, with the result that the outcome can never be predicted from the intention or the tendency of any particular act. The chaotic and unpredictable nature of politics and history is an implication of human freedom and plurality.

It is, therefore, action which bestows significance upon the life of man as a unique individual. Doomed as he is to mortality, he is nevertheless capable of acting and speaking in ways which reveal him as this irreplaceable person, without whom the human world would have been different. This significance, however, is desperately fragile. Unlike the products of a man's hands, his deeds and words do not survive their completion unless they are remembered. Remembrance alone, the retelling of their deeds as stories, can save the lives of men from oblivion and futility; and for this reason the Greeks valued poetry and history, which rescued the glorious deeds of past heroes for the hearing of future generations. Glory is therefore the proper consummation of action, without which its power to save men from futility is lost. Consequently, action is something which is intrinsically a public matter, which cannot be carried on in private but demands the light of common knowledge. Not only is it in any case always carried on in the company of other men, and with reference to their own actions and reactions, but to carry its full significance of revealing the actor and establishing his memory it needs to be made public.

In order to give her view of the human condition vivid embodiment, and also to suggest that it is not without precedent, Hannah Arendt constantly refers in *The Human Condition* to a model of the Greek *polis*, drawn mainly from classical Athens. This serves the purpose of underlining her challenge to contemporary interpretations of politics, for it was in the *polis* that politics was invented; and she has the word of Thucydides' Pericles for it [5] that the very *raison d'être* of the *polis* was to serve action, by providing a public space within which men could reveal themselves for what they were, and a secure remembrance for their actions among the continuing body of the citizens. The *polis* was an association of free citizens, who were sovereign within the private domain of their own households, but who emerged from this privacy and met in the public arena as equals to concern themselves with their common affairs and to seek distinction among their fellows. Within the *polis*, private and public spheres were sharply dissociated. The private realm, the household, was the sphere of necessity. There the slaves whose bondage was the price of their master's liberation from bodily cares laboured to supply his biological needs; there also the women of the household, also subject to biological necessity, laboured to bring forth the next generation. There was no freedom within the household; the master was a despot who ruled by force, a force which merely emphasized the natural necessity under which all lay and from which the master alone was liberated. In order to exercise his freedom, the master had to emerge from the darkness of his private household into the blazing light of the *agora*, the public space where he could move among his equals and vie with them in the pursuit of immortal fame. Here, unlike the household, there was no place for force or despotism: each man was among his equals, and only by persuasion, by the greatness of his words and his example, could he move his fellows and induce them to act with him. Where a tyrant managed to establish himself by force as master of the city, the public realm was simply destroyed as the citizens were banished to the isolation of their own households. The only public activity left under such conditions was the exchange market of the craftsmen, whose concern was with making and not with acting, and whom the Greeks excluded from political life as *banausic*. Politics, the public activity of the *polis*, was characterized by equality, not government; persuasion, not force; freedom, not necessity. Within the household the chief concern was life, biological survival; the business of the public sphere on the other hand was glory, to which life and safety were irrelevant. For this reason, and because acting in public meant revealing oneself for what one was, courage was the pre-eminent political virtue. To the Greeks there was no question but that to be forced to remain in the privacy of the household meant to be deprived of the greatest blessings of human existence; that to be forced to concern oneself only with 'one's own' [6] was 'idiotic' compared with public life.

Hannah Arendt's category of action is so contrary to our ordinary ways of thought, and her whole view of the human condition so unusual, that some readers may be left rather bewildered. In particular, they are likely to want more concrete details about action. What exactly counts as action? What sort of deeds and words is she talking about? What did the men of the Greek *polis do*, and what relation has that to us? It must be confessed that it is hard to give very precise answers to these questions. Reference to the model of the *polis* can give us some help, but not very much. For instance, it is clear that the activities of a man like Pericles, who gained ascendancy in the Athenian democracy and earned himself lasting fame by his capacity for leading his fellow citizens, initiating enterprises and co-ordinating common endeavours, form a paradigm of action that might be applicable unambiguously to some political activities now. On the other hand, Hannah Arendt constantly refers to Achilles, the 'doer of great deeds and speaker of great words'; and whatever Achilles' eloquence in the assembly his fame rested, of course, upon his deeds in battle. Indeed 'great deeds', in the context of the ever-warring Greek *polis*, has an inescapable connotation of personal military valour that seems to suggest that if we are to find more recent parallels, the appropriate place to look might be the Wild West. Contradicting these fighting overtones of the model, however, are the general tone and emphasis of Hannah Arendt's writings, which are not notably warlike. Anything to do with commercial activities, on the other hand, was ruled out by the Greeks as low—although Hannah Arendt does say at one point [7] that the public activities of the market, in which men act in relation to one another, are indeed action.

Hannah Arendt insists that action is a special kind of

activity, quite distinct from the multifarious tasks of earning one's bread or making things, and that politics, when it is action, is something more than a mere offshoot of the social and economic concerns that tend to be seen now as dominating life. It may perhaps help to clarify what she means if we look at a well-known description of a more familiar version of politics—the politics of the 'corridors of power' as described in the novels of C. P. Snow. Snow portrays vividly the world of the higher Civil Service, the ministers and the government scientists, with its manœuvring, alliances, power struggles, personal triumphs and failures. What comes across very clearly is that this restricted world is *the* world for its participants, a world to which, for instance, parliament and the press seem peripheral, and the electorate almost infinitely distant. Furthermore, however much the issues at stake in this world may arise out of the interests and conflicts of society at large, it is clear that within it their main significance is as excuses for the activity of scheming, caballing, steering committees and establishing one's reputation as an able and successful politician. This political activity has a life of its own and is carried on according to laws of its own, almost regardless of the particular issues at stake. Even where questions of the magnitude of nuclear policy are concerned, the political activity goes on in much the same self-contained manner; while Snow has beautifully shown in *The Masters*, his study of an election in a Cambridge college, that precisely the same sort of activities may be carried on with the same intricacy and devotion in cases where an outsider would be at a loss to see that anything was at stake at all. In other words, politics in Snow's sense has two aspects. From the point of view of the outsider, the issues being fought over appear to be the main concern, and he will tend to lay emphasis on the social and economic ones that are to him most comprehensible. But from the point of view of an inhabitant of the political world, the explicit issues are really rather a secondary consideration, and the actual carrying on of politics—influencing committees, winning allies, noting the precise rises and falls in the stock of other politicians and making capital out of them—all this is an end in itself.

We have referred to the politics of Snow's 'corridors of power' because it seems to illuminate some aspects of Hannah

Arendt's concept of action, notably the fact that, in both cases, the emphasis is less on explicit issues and identifiable results than on successes and failures within an elaborate, ingenious, highly competitive game. In both cases, *what* men attempt or achieve is less important than the activity itself. All the same, we must not take the comparison too far, for it is very doubtful whether Hannah Arendt would accept Snow's committee men as paradigms of action in her sense. They differ from her own models, the citizens of the Greek *polis* or the leaders of the American Revolution, in two particularly important respects: in the first place they are experts, differentiated from the rest of the community by bureaucratic training and expertise, whereas Hannah Arendt constantly has in mind a democracy of all free citizens; and in the second place their activities are secret from the point of view of the community at large, whereas Hannah Arendt insists that action must be public. It is possible, indeed, to argue that neither of these differences is so great as it might seem. The free citizens of the Greek *polis*, for instance, also constituted an élite with political training and experience compared with the bulk of the population (women, slaves and foreign residents); while, as regards the question of publicity, not *all* the activities of, say, the American Founding Fathers were carried on in the full glare of democratic daylight, and that devious politician Benjamin Franklin would fit admirably into the world of Snow's novels. Snow's political circle is a world of its own within which political activities are indeed carried on in public in the sense that they are closely watched by the other members; it is also an arena in which men seek glory. There is perhaps, therefore, less difference than one might expect between the two conceptions, although the genuine difference that does exist is manifest in Hannah Arendt's belief that political activity should be available to far more people than the present élite, a hope quite alien to the meritocratic tone of Snow's novels.

There is another difference of emphasis that is perhaps particularly revealing. Snow's men are by no means automata or the tools of social and economic forces; the outcome of their manœuvrings is by no means predictable; nevertheless they act very much as participants in a tradition, playing an established game according to the rules. In Hannah Arendt's case, however, the emphasis is above all on the power of men to start new things, to *begin*. She lays great stress on the inherently unpredictable nature of action, which consists in beginnings and their unforeseeable outcomes, and it is entirely in keeping with this that most of the concrete modern examples of action that she discusses are cases of revolution or rebellion. She talks, for instance, of the American Revolution, the Paris Commune of 1870, the creation of Soviets in the Russian Revolutions, the French Resistance to Hitler and the Hungarian Revolt of 1956. In all these cases individual men had the courage to stop behaving in a routine manner, to step forward from their private lives to create a public space and to act within it in such a way that, while the memory of their actions lasts, the human world can never again be as if they had not existed. In doing so, according to Hannah Arendt, they rediscovered the truth known to the Greeks, that action is the supreme blessing that bestows significance upon individual human life. In *On Revolution* she devotes much attention to this rediscovery by the men of the American Revolution, the Founding Fathers, who might pretend in obedience to traditional values that they longed for private life and only engaged in politics from a sense of duty, but who made it clear in their letters and recollections that they had discovered unexpected delights in action upon the public stage, and had acquired the taste for freedom, for earning distinction among their equals. She quotes from John Adams, for instance, a view of the evils of poverty that could only come from one who had tasted the splendours of public life:

The poor man's conscience is clear; yet he is ashamed. . . . He feels himself out of the sight of others, groping in the dark. Mankind takes no notice of him. . . . In the midst of a crowd, at church, in the market . . . he is in as much obscurity as he would be in a garret or a cellar. He is not disapproved, censured, or reproached; *he is only not seen*. . . . To be wholly overlooked, and to know it, are intolerable.[8]

Again, in *Between Past and Future* [9] she quotes the French poet, René Char, on the experience of acting in the Resistance to Hitler, and how what had at first seemed a burden turned out to be a treasure, the 'world of reality' from which peace banished them into the 'sad opaqueness' of private life.

65

POLITICS AND THE HUMAN CONDITION

Hannah Arendt's understanding of the human condition shows us man not only as labourer and worker but above all as a unique individual who exercises his freedom and reveals his individual self in action, in starting things, gaining distinction among his fellows, and doing what no one, not even he himself, could safely predict. This picture is clearly directed against the views of human life current today, and especially against the sociological understanding of men not as unique individuals but as occupants of social roles or members of social groups who behave in regular and predictable ways. Her claim is that even now men are capable of free action, but that this requires for its setting a public space constituted by equals who are aware of their own freedom, and for most people in the modern world this is lacking. Further, she claims that the point of politics is precisely to provide such a public space for action. This was the origin of politics in the Greek *polis*, and this is still its true *raison d'être*. In this section we shall be looking in more detail at what this conception of politics involves and how it differs from our current assumptions.

Perhaps the first point to be underlined is that her views utterly contradict modern assumptions about the proper purpose of politics. Liberals have long maintained that the function of politics is to protect and reconcile the private interests of the members of the community; and sociologists, Marxian and otherwise, have long added the gloss that politics not only ought to be but inevitably is the outcome of social interests and conflicts, and that it is in fact a superstructure upon society, possessing little autonomy and largely determined by social changes. Hannah Arendt disputes both the claim that politics always *is* simply an offshoot of society, and also the view that this is what it *ought* to be; and she goes further by challenging the whole concept of 'society'. We shall have occasion later to look in more detail at her views on this question. She points out that the concept of 'society' was unknown to the Greeks, who knew only the distinction between the private household, the realm of necessity, and the public space of the *polis*, the realm of freedom. For them there could be no question but that the private existed for the sake of the public, to make free action possible, and not the public for the sake of the private. It is this ancient distinction between public and private that has, she claims, been lost since the time of the Greeks in the all-embracing category of the 'social'. Already when Thomas Aquinas translated Aristotle's political terms into medieval Latin, he transposed Aristotle's claim that man is a political animal, with its overtones of the public life of the *polis*, into 'Man is by nature political, that is social'.[10] In subsequent political theory the Greek understanding of politics, as a free activity which is *unnatural*, superimposed upon nature and its necessities, was replaced by a new understanding of man as naturally social, needing the company of other men for the purposes of biological life and creating political organizations simply as a means to serve these purposes. In other words, where the ancient world had thought of the household, the realm of economy, as existing for the sake of politics in order to free citizens for the higher life of action, most of our tradition of political theory has taken for granted that politics exists for the sake of society, while society is a sort of inflated family household comprising all members of the community and concerned with the needs of life. The Marxist claim that politics should not be seen as an independent activity but as a superstructure upon socio-economic interest seems to her no special discovery of Karl Marx, but the common assumption of virtually all political theory and political economy of the modern age. Consequently politics is no longer seen as the realm of freedom but as determined by 'social forces', imagined as working with the same necessity as physical ones. This view of politics seems to her to be quite inadequate for understanding political situations even in the modern world—for instance the American Revolution—in which individual men *have* acted in unforeseeable ways to make new beginnings; and also pernicious, in that it can lead men to disbelieve in their own freedom, and, even when placed in situations where free action is open to them, to behave like robots following what they believe to be the dictates of necessity. One of the most weird features of totalitarianism, according to her account of it, is that its leaders, while turning the world of their subjects upside-down, apparently understood what they were doing not as a gigantic exercise of human arbitrariness but as the mere working out of an ideology to its logical conclusion. But for Hannah Arendt politics has the peculiar dignity of being the *locus* of freedom, the public space in which action is possible, so that to see it merely as a social superstructure or a mechanism for balancing interests seems to her a terrible loss to human existence.

One striking aspect of her view of politics as action is that it appears to exclude government, rule, force and sovereignty— for many of us, if asked for an off-the-cuff definition of politics, would give an answer in these very terms. Her contention, reinforced by her model of the Greek *polis*, is that force and rulership are *prepolitical*: politics starts where they leave off.[11] There were government, sovereignty and force to spare in the Greek household, but there was no politics in her sense. Politics existed in the public space constituted by the free and equal masters of households. Her point is of course not merely the etymological one that our term 'politics' comes originally from experiences other than rulership and administration, but rather that when we use it and the rest of our political vocabulary to describe government we have no terms left for the experience of action among equals, and are liable to forget even the possibility of such action, and to take for granted that the hierarchical relation between government and subjects is the only possible mode in which human beings can live together.

Together with our common emphasis on government as an inevitable feature of politics goes our usual assumption that politics is essentially a matter of the working of political institutions. Against this, Hannah Arendt sets the view that all that is necessary for the existence of politics is a public space in which men can meet as equals and begin to act. Such a public space may be defined by permanent institutions, but it may also spring into being in a completely informal way—most dramatically among those involved in a revolution; more humbly, among neighbours roused to demonstrate against the siting of an airport on their doorsteps, or among members of a community who grow exasperated with official inactivity over housing and begin to act together to change things themselves: the possibilities are infinite. In each of these cases, whatever the particular purpose or occasion that brought them together, those involved find themselves constituting a public space with its own common life, within which they participate not as rulers and subjects but as equals who find their relative positions only by merit gained in the eyes of their fellows. Such public spaces can spring up unpredictably from nowhere and just as unpredictably disappear again. The importance of institutions to politics is in providing some more or less permanent framework to shelter and preserve the public arena for future generations and to restrain the unpredictability of action within minimum limits. Hannah Arendt remarks in *The Human Condition* [12] that the Greeks saw the laws of the city-state in the image of a wall which defined, bounded and protected the public space that was the *polis*. Legislation was therefore part of the foundation of cities, a necessary activity, but not itself a political one, and one which outsiders, strangers to the *polis*, were often called in to fulfil. Lawmaking, in fact, like the building of the physical walls of the city, did not belong to the category of action but to that of work, craftsmanship. Precisely because politics and the public space in which it is carried on are so fragile, the work of constitution-building is necessary to supplement them.

Hannah Arendt claims, then, that many of our common assumptions about politics obscure rather than illuminate precisely what is specific to the political realm. She suggests that one of the main sources of this confusion is that politics has so often been envisaged in terms of work, of making, rather than of action. Plato, the originator of the whole Western tradition of political philosophy, started this when he opposed to the Athenian democracy of all free citizens the model of the craftsman who is an expert in his trade and therefore fitted to tell others what to do, and who works with the idea of his end product before his eyes, subordinating his material to the achievement of this end. Plato drew up the first Utopia, a blueprint of a city in which all would be ordered according to the model, rulership exercised by those who could understand it, and politics, in the sense of free action in public, utterly banished. The activity of work, of making, demands a unity of purpose in the adjustment of means to ends that can only be achieved either in solitude or by the rule of one man over others. Wherever politics has been visualized in the image of making something—as in many revolutionary theories—the implication of the need for central direction, unified sovereignty, naturally follows. So also does the need for violent transformation of the given 'material', always part of the activity of fabrication. Action is the very opposite of work in being inherently unpredictable and disorderly, by virtue of the plurality and freedom of those who engage in it; order and predictability in gaining predetermined ends can be achieved only at the expense of plurality and freedom. Hannah Arendt maintains that the notion of sovereignty can have no place in politics understood in its proper category of action. Where men act as plural individuals, some of them may be conspicuous for strength of body or mind, and together they can generate power, but sovereignty, with its connotations of unified control over the outcome of events, is impossible. Sovereignty is consistent only with the death of politics and its replacement by government. She considers that our tradition of political theory has erred disastrously in supposing that freedom implies sovereignty, that only he whose command over his actions and their outcome is sovereign can be free:

If it were true that sovereignty and freedom are the same, then indeed no man could be free, because sovereignty, the ideal of uncompromising self-sufficiency and mastership, is contradictory to the very condition of plurality. No man can be sovereign because not one man, but men, inhabit the earth.[13]

If sovereignty is, according to Hannah Arendt, incompatible with politics, power emphatically is not, and since she uses the term unusually it is necessary to go into what she means by it and the distinctions with which she sets it about. It is contrasted with violence on the one hand and with strength on the other. Violence is self-explanatory: its significance here lies in her insistence that power does not consist of nor rest upon violence, and can indeed quite often defeat it. The exercise of violence may be able on the other hand to destroy power, but it cannot generate it, and tyrannies resting simply upon violence not only reduce their subjects to impotence but condemn themselves to the same fate. If power is not an outcome of violence, neither is it a product of strength. By strength Hannah Arendt means the individual gifts of mind or body belonging to particular men. Men vary greatly in the strength with which they are endowed by nature, but strength does not itself produce power, and the power of a group of men acting together is in no way proportionate to their strength as separate individuals. Power is in fact the energy which is generated by men acting together, which may be out of all proportion to their individual strength or their means of violence. The common political phenomenon of a small group acting so vigorously together that, most improbably, they defeat what appear to be overwhelming forces arrayed against them, is a phenomenon of power. The victory of revolutionaries over established governments is often due to a combination of the impotence of the old regime, in spite of its weapons of violence, and the new power generated by small numbers of men who have begun to act together. Modern movements of civil disobedience and passive resistance demonstrate that great power may be generated with no recourse to violence at all, simply by virtue of common action. The power vanishes again just as quickly if the actors are dispersed, either by being defeated by force and frightened into isolation or by drifting apart into their private lives.

It is in *On Revolution*,[14] in the course of her discussion of the American Revolution and the problems of founding the Republic, that Hannah Arendt discusses power in most detail, and makes clear that it is something which should not be viewed negatively, as a quality that governments automatically possess and that needs to be limited, but positively: any body politic needs power, and must find ways of generating this positive energy, for which violence is no substitute. Since power is a positive energy, there is no foreseeable limit to the amount of it that can be generated, and balancing powers, establishing various centres of power over against one another, does not necessarily divide or weaken power, but may increase it by mutual stimulation. The American Republic was more, not less, powerful with centres of power at both state and federal level than it would have been if more centralized. Furthermore, contrary to the common liberal assumption, Hannah Arendt considers that power and freedom are not opposites, such that to increase freedom one must always check power; on the contrary, power and freedom belong together as positive and interdependent political phenomena.[15]

Another political issue which Hannah Arendt's approach sets in a new light is the question of property and its justification. She discusses it in *The Human Condition* in the context of the Greek *polis*. There, the privacy of property was correlative to the publicity of political life. Possession of a piece of property was a condition of citizenship. However, this property was not disposable nor at the will of its owner: it was a sacred family possession which provided the citizen with a permanent location in the world. According to her custom, Hannah Arendt articulates the meaning of property by means of a distinction between property and wealth. By property she means a privately owned place in the world; by wealth an abundance of consumable goods. Prior to the modern age, property was invariably sacred, its boundaries protected by special gods and its centre the hearth with its household divinities, whereas wealth, she says, has become sacred only in the modern world. The accumulation of wealth since the sixteenth century has proceeded largely by means of the destruction of permanent property, starting with the expropriation of the peasants with their ancient rights in village land. She notes that Proudhon, while stigmatizing capitalist property as 'theft', nevertheless recognized the protective functions of private property; and she suggests that he was looking for just such a distinction between wealth and property as she proposes. In the modern world, private accumulation of wealth—like a process of nature, an apparently irresistible and automatic process—has nowhere respected property, and has consumed it as almost all other elements of a durable world have been consumed. What we have lost is 'a privately owned place to hide in'[16]—a hiding-place which she thinks of as just as necessary to human life as a public space in which to act: the two are dialectically related. Consequently modern arguments between socialists and liberals about whether or not property should be respected seem to her largely meaningless, since the pseudo-automatic processes of developing industry, increasing productivity and expanding wealth have already destroyed the permanence and security that had always been the essence and justification of property.

It is time to turn explicitly to Hannah Arendt's understanding of freedom, which is perhaps her most significant contribution to political theory. All her work is pervaded by her emphasis

on the possibility of freedom, which is more or less equivalent
to action and hence to politics. Her understanding of the term
is by no means without precedent—de Tocqueville and Montesquieu are precursors whom she occasionally acknowledges—
but there can be no denying that it is contrary to the main
body of current and traditional usage. When we speak of
freedom we most commonly mean to refer to the situation of
an individual who is to some degree an island defended
against the world. We think of him as not being bound or
imprisoned, not being interfered with, being able to treat his
home as his castle, being able to think and worship as he
chooses and to perform self-regarding actions without having
the rest of society breathing down the back of his neck. When
we consider the notion of freedom more deeply we commonly
find ourselves entangled in questions about the extent to which
any individual can be as detached from others as the image
demands, and about how even within his own mind and
character pressures operate upon him through conditioning
and motives to stop him being 'really' free. Generally speaking
there is no doubt that our ordinary thinking about freedom,
both our certainties and our perplexities, has a great deal in
common with that of John Stuart Mill; and our basic assumption, like his, is that the less other people interfere with us the
freer we are.

Against this almost universally accepted view that freedom
is a feature of private life, Hannah Arendt sets the totally
opposed notion that it is located in public life and is a feature
of action carried on in the company of one's fellows.[17] Freedom
is positive, not at all in T. H. Green's sense of the victory of
conscience over inclination, but in the sense that it lies in the
experience of acting in public, not of being left alone in
private. Before considering the validity or otherwise of this
proposed change in terminology, it is necessary to make quite
clear the kind of experiences that Hannah Arendt is talking
about, the context in which they are set and the alternatives
with which they are contrasted. Her crucial distinction here is
that between freedom and liberation. It is a feature of the
human condition that man lives both as part of nature, subject
to the determinism of natural forces, and as an unnatural being
who transforms nature, creates new things and acts in ways

that are not dictated by biological need. Man is both an unfree being in so far as he is part of nature and subject to natural necessity, and free in so far as he can superimpose upon nature his own human world and its web of new, man-created words and deeds. Where nature is endlessly predictable, man alone is constitutionally capable of new beginnings. Indeed, Hannah Arendt is fond of pointing out that from the standpoint of nature and its regular, predictable, automatic processes, men constantly perform miracles—she often quotes Saint Augustine's remark that man was created in order that there might be a beginning.[18] A precondition of this freedom is that those who are to partake of it should be in some degree *liberated* from the burden of nature, as for instance the citizens of the Greek *polis* were liberated by their possession of slaves. But this liberation does not in itself constitute freedom: it only makes it possible. The citizen who sits at home, watching his slaves work for him (or drawing the income from his investments) is liberated to some extent from nature's determination, but he is not free, for he is not exercising his potential freedom. Where he and others are kept at home by the fear of a tyrant who has substituted his own rule for the public realm, then liberation from the force of the tyrant (which metaphorically resembles the force of nature) is also necessary before freedom can be enjoyed. But, again, mere liberation, the mere banishing of the tyrant, is only a condition for freedom: freedom itself does not exist until the citizens are acting together, starting new things and making a name for themselves.

We shall have occasion to look again at Hannah Arendt's distinction between freedom and liberation when we discuss her reflections *On Revolution*. Briefly, however, her contention is that revolutions have commonly been started for the sake of freedom, for the sake of participating in the public sphere and exercising the human faculty for making beginnings, and that in their early stages this freedom has been enjoyed by the participants: but that in all modern revolutions subsequent to the American the impulse for freedom or admission to the public realm has been swamped by the desire of the masses for liberation from the necessities of nature, and that in hopeless efforts to effect this liberation the revolutionary leaders replaced freedom with tyranny. Nevertheless she insists that the initial aim of the French Revolution, and the triumphant experience of the American Revolution, was freedom, 'public freedom':

> Their public freedom was not an inner realm into which men might escape at will from the pressures of the world, nor was it the *liberum arbitrium* which makes the will choose between alternatives. Freedom for them could exist only in public; it was a tangible, worldly reality, something created by men to be enjoyed by men rather than a gift or capacity, it was the man-made public space or market-place which antiquity had known as the area where freedom appears and becomes visible to all.[19]

The point about this desire for a chance to act significantly in public is that it is only likely to be appreciated by those who are already liberated from the overwhelming pressure of bodily need and from the human bondage of slavery to a master. It demands as a prerequisite that those who are to partake of it already enjoy physical sufficiency and civil liberties, and it has therefore always been a minority considera-tion, liable to be lost in the longing of the mass of men for deliverance from need and bondage. Nevertheless it seems to Hannah Arendt an amazing vindication of the human taste for freedom and of man's constant capacity to do the miracu-lously unexpected that in the century since the Paris Com-mune, movements for immediate participation in public affairs, for the founding of Soviets, communes or workers' councils, have sprung up among the working classes in every revolution, always defeated by party bureaucracies but constantly revived. In such impulses to the foundation of grass-roots democracy, the exercise of freedom by ordinary men and women, she sees the most hopeful sign of a possible salvation of mankind from atrophy in mass society and bureaucracy.

It would, we believe, be pointless to try to evaluate her position on the assumption that there can only be one proper use of the term 'freedom', and that either she or else J. S. Mill and most of our tradition is wrong about it. There can be no doubt that Mill and other liberals have articulated experiences that have general validity and significance (so of course did T. H. Green, although the experiences he talked about were different from Mill's); and we see no reason to doubt that Hannah Arendt also has given expression to a range of experiences that, while of necessity less common than those available in private life, are the constant concomitants of political action, although they have been remarkably neglected in our tradition of political thought.[20] Particularly at present, when so many rather muddled attempts are being made to articulate the notion of 'participation', there seems every reason to be grateful for her clarity in describing the adventure of sharing in public affairs. Her own emphasis is of course very strongly in favour of public freedom, and critical of mere liberation and the enjoyment of private life—but whether or not one is prepared to go along with her scale of priorities, it is illuminating to have a long-unarticulated (although quite commonly experienced) good brought back before one's eyes.

COMMENTS

In this chapter we have endeavoured to give an account of the centre of Hannah Arendt's thought, her understanding of the human condition and the view of politics that goes with it, notably her concept of action and concomitant understanding of freedom. Her views are original and interesting, but they are also in some ways puzzling and open to objection. We do not propose to try to sit in judgment on her theory, but merely to attempt in this final section to articulate some of the problems that spring to mind in connection with the views we have been expounding.

The first problem we have touched on already, namely that of determining just what is to count as falling within the category of action. Her view that human beings need, to bestow significance upon their individual existence, some public space where they can act and make a name for themselves among their equals is undoubtedly an interesting one; but we may question how large scale this public space needs to be. The *polis* is an illuminating model, but one that is difficult to compare with present-day conditions in that it was both a state, carrying on what is conventionally called politics as well as warfare, and at the same time a face-to-face community in which the citizens had the chance to know one another personally. Hannah Arendt seems to take for granted that the only possible public space that could be available nowadays must be that in which politics at state level is carried on, and deplores the size, centralization and bureaucracy of modern states. But would it be stretching her concepts improperly to suggest that public spaces for action are in fact to be found all over our communities, in the shape of organizations and gatherings of all kinds, political and non-political; and that in churches, public houses, bowling clubs and women's institutes as well as political direct action groups people find places where they can act, begin things, distinguish themselves among their peers and leave a name behind them? It may be objected that what individuals do in these situations is trivial because it cannot enable them to control the conditions of their lives; but according to Hannah Arendt it is foolish to expect this even from politics—action is not a sovereign activity, and does not enable one to *control* one's own life, only to make one's mark upon the common world.

Again, when Hannah Arendt talks of politics as action how much of what we ordinarily call 'politics' is she including? Clearly, her category is narrower than that of common speech. For instance, we often talk about the internal 'politics' of organizations or groups, when we mean to refer to the struggles for power, the manœuvring and manipulating, the forming of alliances and striking of bargains that go on behind the scenes almost everywhere, whatever the official hierarchy of command. As we noted when comparing Hannah Arendt with C. P. Snow, this kind of activity has certain things in common with Hannah Arendt's action. It is carried on, if not among those who are formally equal, at any rate among those who recognize one another as having influence and being possible allies to be courted or opponents to be defeated; its outcome is unpredictable, proceeding from the interactions of many contributors in such a way as to produce 'political solutions' that can cause great embarrassment when an attempt has to be made to justify them rationally in public; it is certainly an activity that is loved for its own sake, becoming something of an addiction to those who find that they have a talent for it, so that they will often devote to it energy quite disproportionate to the issue supposedly at stake. It differs from action, in fact, mainly in the requirement of publicity that is built into the latter: for behind-the-scenes politics, like diplomacy, would lose its very nature by being carried on in public.

It is perhaps partly because of this requirement of publicity that Hannah Arendt is so unwilling to regard most of modern party politics as true politics, action in a public space. Where the public deliberations of a parliament, and the public speeches of politicians, are generally considered to be chiefly exercises in window-dressing, while most of the real business goes on in secret within party machines and pressure-groups, politics in her sense is not present. However, her rejection of party politics goes much deeper than this. She is prepared to admit that the two-party system in the United States and Great Britain works in some slight degree, providing a public space of sorts for a few politicians and representing the interests of the people, thereby providing some check on government; what it does *not* do is to provide any opportunity for action for the vast majority of the citizens, whose only way into politics is via the party machines which select career-politicians.[21] But it is clear that her views on party politics have not in any case been formed on the basis of Britain and America, and that when she thinks of parliamentary politics in general with such unmitigated contempt what she has in mind are the shaky multi-party systems of continental Europe since the First World War. She considers such parties as the greatest enemies of action, being bureaucratic, doctrinaire and intolerant of opposition,[22] and she sees only differences of fortune between one-party dictatorships and multi-party systems. It is perhaps arguable that this is a case where her continental European background gives her thought a cast which limits its relevance to Britain and America; certainly her dismissal of party politics and her enthusiasm for workers' councils have a flavour about them which is oddly remote from Anglo-Saxon experience. We shall have occasion later in the book to discuss her views on revolutionary councils; for the present we are concerned simply to note that when she talks of action and politics she evidently has in mind such councils rather than parties, and revolutionary spontaneity rather than parliamentary procedure. Indeed one doubt that may perhaps arise in the minds of readers who value order is whether a community in which action in her sense was widespread might not be too anarchic to be comfortable. Action, which constantly starts new things and sets off processes beyond control, is not conducive to peace and quiet, and seems indeed to suggest permanent revolution, if of a brand very different from the Communist kind.

Some readers will find the greatest stumbling-block in Hannah Arendt's political thought her apparent lack of concern for economic and social equality. Many people of goodwill, reading what she has to say about political freedom and the life of action—especially that the Greeks were able to enjoy it because they had slaves, and that the French revolutionaries were dragged down from it by the needs of the poor —will undoubtedly feel that she has got her priorities wrong, and that she ought to agree that the relief of poverty is more urgent than the establishment of political freedom. Similar questions have, of course, been argued many times before, notably between Western liberals and communists in the 1930s; and it is perhaps enough to remark that where more or less socialist ways of thinking and notions of priority are so dominant in thought and rhetoric (if hardly in actions and results) Hannah Arendt needs no excuse for emphasizing other, less generally admitted, values. Her theory can perhaps be called élitist in the sense that her main concern is for those, perhaps always the few, who are able and willing to summon up the energy to act—although it is also radically democratic in its critique of parliamentary institutions that limit the opportunity for action to career politicians.

A final point which may cause some disquiet is her claim that action cannot be judged by moral standards. She says that

action can be judged only by the criterion of greatness because it is in its nature to break through the commonly accepted and reach into the extraordinary.[23]

And she quotes Thucydides' Pericles to the effect that the glory of Athens consisted in having left behind 'everywhere everlasting remembrance of their good and their evil deeds'. Some readers, confronted with this assurance that action aims at glory and not at goodness, may be inclined to wonder whether the world would be the better for more of it, and whether the evils that, according to Hannah Arendt, our belief in necessity has brought upon us might not have been equalled by men exercising their freedom in action.

4

The Modern World

In the last chapter we looked at Hannah Arendt's picture of human nature and the human situation, or rather of those aspects of it that seem to her in danger of being forgotten and in need of reassertion. We saw that she chose to connect this picture closely with a vanished age of human life, the age of ancient Greece, and that she did so in order to contrast it with the modern world as a kind of norm from which the latter has departed. In this chapter we shall be investigating the second half of this contrast—her analysis of modernity, its causes and its defects. This attempt to comprehend the situation in which mankind now finds itself, 'to think what we are doing', as she puts it,[1] is in fact the central concern of all her writing to which she returns again and again. We have already seen her following one such line of investigation in *The Origins of Totalitarianism*; others appear in *The Human Condition*, in *On Revolution* and in her essays, notably the brilliant essay on 'The Concept of History'.[2] In *The Human Condition* she prefaces her examination of modernity and its origins with her model of normal human life from which the modern world has diverged: and we have been able to present that model in a fairly systematic way, because, although she adds variations in other essays, she has only given the one full-length description. Where her investigations of modernity are concerned, however, we must follow a different procedure, because, in spite of the constant recurrence of similar themes and the overlapping of ideas, each of her studies of the modern world follows a different train of thought. To concoct out of these separate acts of reflection a systematic doctrine that would somehow comprehend them all would be quite artificial, besides giving a misleading impression of her mode of thought; so in this chapter we shall be looking separately at the analyses she gives, each time from a rather different viewpoint, in the latter part of *The Human Condition,* in *On Revolution* and in 'The Concept of History'. Before proceeding to her particular accounts, however, we can profitably discuss two concepts of hers that are crucial to all her discussions. In all her analyses of modernity, one of her primary intentions is to make us aware of its oddity, to make us look at our age critically instead of taking it for granted as the normal state of human life. In order to achieve this end she has developed a number of critical concepts which we shall encounter again and again. 'Process' and 'Life' are among them, as we shall see, but those that will perhaps most immediately repay our study are 'The World' (and its correlative, 'Worldlessness') and 'Society' (taken to its logical conclusion in 'Mass Society').

THE WORLD [3]

To talk about men in modern times as Worldless, as Hannah Arendt constantly does, may strike us as odd and unintelligible. She is concerned, however, to make a point about the human condition in general as well as about modernity in particular, and to challenge the widespread assumption that what is wrong with life now is that men's situation has become 'unnatural' in some way. 'The World' as a category is set directly in opposition to nature. When Hannah Arendt talks about the world she does not mean the physical world: indeed the world in her view is precisely what separates and shields man from nature. It is the human artifice of man-made objects and institutions that provides human beings with a permanent home. Civilization, which has made man something more than an animal, has consisted precisely in the building of this world, a world of ploughed fields, roads and hedges instead of wild landscape, of buildings instead of the open air, of language and culture, communities and traditions, of art, law, religion and all the rest of the man-made things that nevertheless outlive the men who made them and form the inheritance of the human race. We have seen her beginning in *The Origins of Totalitarianism* to reflect upon this contrast between the human world and nature: when she considered the differences between the Africans, who had made so little impact upon nature, and the Europeans who had made so much; and also when she reflected upon the displaced persons who found themselves thrust back into a 'state of nature', without rights, when there was no artificial human community to own them. How fragile but how necessary to human life this super-natural human world is. In order to live a human life we need more than nature. Nature moves in endless cycles of growth and decay, and of course in so far as we are organic beings we do so too; but, being men, we are able to save ourselves from this futility of nature by building an artificial world to house us. This world, though it must be constantly guarded against nature's processes of attrition, will then remain stable and outlast each individual life, providing a solid background against which the significance of each individual life will be visible. Without such a stable human world our lives cannot form significant stories, but only be part of the endless flux of nature.

Hannah Arendt points out that such a stable world is an essential condition of a fully human life; she suggests in particular that it is the necessary basis for proper thinking, judging and acting, because the world we have in common can alone provide a touchstone of reality. As we have already seen in *The Origins of Totalitarianism* it seems to her that ideological styles of thought and their acceptance by masses in modern times is a sign that those who accept them have been driven back on their own mental resources and deprived of the common sense which only a stable community can provide. She has elaborated this suggestion in *The Human Condition* and elsewhere. She points out that experiences that are private lack the stamp of reality. Not only dreams, but also such intense but non-public experiences as pain and suffering have a quality of unreality compared with our awareness of things that are there amongst us all for all to see and touch and move round. Private experiences, however intense, are subjective, whereas the standard of reality is supplied by our objective experiences of those objects that are there for all of us continuously. And one of the striking things about this common world is that we all see the same things from different viewpoints. Men have a common awareness of reality, not when they are all seeing and thinking in identical ways, but, on the contrary, when they are all seeing and thinking about the same objects (whether physical or spiritual objects) from their own different points of view. Where there is a stable world of objects and institutions each man, looking at it from his own point of view, will supplement every other man's point of view, providing them all with a rich and concrete sense of reality: and, above all, the objective world will provide a standard against which to judge the subjectivity of private imaginings. In other words, according to Hannah Arendt, where a stable common world exists, men have the necessary, in fact indispensable, basis for common sense. Clearly, part of the essential nature of such a world, if it is to house us and provide us with a standard of reality, is that it should be durable and fairly permanent. It will of course change, but it should change gradually and imperceptibly, so that the men who live in it experience it as being more durable than themselves. Where, as in modern times, the world is in a condition of constant transformation it cannot provide a stable dwelling-place for man, and he therefore finds himself in a condition of worldlessness that threatens his security, deprives his life of significance and destroys his common sense of reality.

For a proper human world to exist it is necessary for men to recognize that they have obligations to it. The world is something that men have in common, but in the nature of things its life transcends theirs. It is their common heritage, the context that gives their individual lives significance, but something which has interests of its own over and above theirs. Like the estate and mansion of an ancient family (to import a Burkean image that Hannah Arendt herself does not use) it gives the individual who inherits it a place, a dignity and a significance, but it also makes demands upon him, it has interests that he must serve perhaps at the expense of his own life interests, as a nobleman might stint himself to pass on a glorified estate to his successors, or plant trees in his park that only his grandchildren would see grown to full stature. Hannah Arendt discusses an example of this point in her recent essay, *On Violence*, in talking about the fallacies of 'enlightened self-interest'. She mentions the constant conflict of interests in modern cities over rented accommodation, where 'enlightened self-interest' would seem to demand a building fit for human habitation—which surely ought in the long run to be better for landlord and tenant alike. But actually the interest of the landlord in high profit and of the tenant in low rent coincide in the will to let the building fall into decay: it is not *their* interest, but the interest of the world, that demands rebuilding of the house:

Self-interest is interested in the self, and the self dies or moves out or sells the house; because of its changing condition, that is, ultimately, because of the human condition of mortality, the self *qua* self cannot reckon in terms of long-range interest, i.e. the interest of a world that survives its inhabitants.[4]

The capacity that makes a human world possible, that created and sustains it, is work, man's activity as *Homo faber*. In work, of which the creation of works of art is the paradigm case, man strives to create something that will outlive him, to add another permanent object to the human artifice. The classic standards by which his product is judged—according to its beauty, its utility and its durability—are 'worldly' standards, considering whether or not it is fit to belong to the world. In creating an object, the craftsman defies man's mortality by showing that at any rate the work of human hands can be deathless. It is not only in the realm of material objects that such a concept is relevant, for from the time of the Romans onwards one of the dominant themes of political life was the desire to build a political structure that would have this same power of survival, and Rome itself, Sparta and the Venetian Republic attracted the admiration of such secularly minded political theorists as Machiavelli simply because of their durability. Ever since the fall of Rome, however, the conception of earthly immortality embodied in a world of permanent objects, including a public realm that would preserve the memory of its founders, has been challenged by the Christian belief in eternal life for the individual soul. The Christians, proselytizing among the ruins of the ancient world, stressed the frailty of everything worldly, and urged their followers to turn away from the world and all its values to the quest for individual salvation in eternity. According to Hannah Arendt, the modern age is in the position of having lost this faith in eternal life, while at the same time losing the durable world that can provide earthly immortality. She diagnoses the condition of modern man as Worldlessness, a condition in which every individual, lacking a world common to him and others, is thrown back upon his own inner life, while all that unites him with his fellows is the common rhythm of the life of the species. Modern man, therefore, instead of living with others a fully human life in a world common to all of them, lives partly within his own mind, cut off from others, and partly as a member of his species, united with other men by sheer animal needs.

SOCIETY [5]

Connected with Hannah Arendt's analysis of worldlessness in modern life is another critical concept, 'Society'. It may seem strange to find society treated as a critical concept, when we normally take for granted that society is simply there under all circumstances of human life. But Hannah Arendt's purpose is precisely to criticize this assumption. To think of her as a theorist of Mass Society is misleading, since she claims that one of the significant features of the groups in which men live now is not just that they are *mass* societies but that they are societies at all: she uses the term not as a generic one applying to all human groups, but with a specific meaning. Her claim is that 'society' constitutes a new and specifically modern mode of organized living together, in which men are united only by their common membership of the human species and the care for survival that they share, not by a common human world and a public realm of action. She contrasts this situation with the ancient distinction between the public realm of the city and the private realm of the household, and suggests that modern society is a sort of inflated form of the ancient household, in which also the dominant cares were those of biological life. The very term 'economy', which comes from the Greek word for household and originally meant housekeeping, now denotes the predominant activities of society as a whole. Like the members of a family, modern men are related to one another by their common biological nature and cares— although of course without the corresponding personal ties. Characteristic of society, she claims, is the lack of distance between men that a public world provides, so that instead of appearing as distinct individuals against the background of a common world, men appear in society as members who are expected to conform, to share a common interest, and to *behave* predictably, not *act* individually. She seems to consider that society in this sense of stifling conformity first existed in the 'polite society' of modern Europe, for instance the world of the salons against whose pressures Rousseau reacted so violently, and that Rousseau's attempt to preserve the intimacy of the heart against these social pressures was characteristic of the problems raised by the existence of society in modern times.

Her suggestion, then, is that men in modern society live together in much the same way as the members of the ancient family (except for the head of the household) used to do: dominated by biological needs, having one common interest represented by the head of the household, and united in a strict conformity that had no room for individualism. She suggests that the modern disintegration of the patriarchal family is but part and parcel of its absorption into social groups, of which the political expression has been the nation-state. The nation-state started with a form of government, absolute monarchy, which was the direct analogy of the patriarchal family, but has developed very naturally towards bureaucracy, which Hannah Arendt calls 'rule by nobody'— the replacement of government by administration of the collective society in the assumed common interest, finally excluding any responsibility or any kind of action or individual freedom. For a time, in the nineteenth century, the social groups into which the family had been absorbed were social classes; now these classes have themselves been subsumed in the modern mass society in which every individual is identified only by his function. It seems to her an indication of the extent to which society has replaced the public realm of action that the modern academic world is dominated by the 'behavioural' social sciences, which are concerned precisely with behaviour and not with action. Action, deeds and events are individual, singular matters, unpredictable and not susceptible of statistical treatment, although they alone give meaning to life and above all to history. Statistics are relevant only to behaviour, which is characteristic of social man, who participates in the process of biological life and fulfils his function without deviation. Her fear is not that the findings of the behavioural sciences are false, but that they are becoming only too true as men become more exclusively social beings. Similarly she suggests that Marxist predictions of the coming of 'socialized man', the 'withering away of the state' and the replacement of government by administration have proved well founded, except that the enthusiasm with which Marx and Engels viewed this prospect was misplaced. She claims [6] that 'through society it is the life process itself which in one form or another has been channeled into the public realm', and the replacement of action and work by labour, the most 'natural' of human activities, is part of the same process. The problem is not that modern society is unnatural, but that it is too close to nature to be fully human. Social man, now not even a member of a family or a class but only of a mass, is united with his fellows by their common nature, but not by any common human artificial world that would gather them together while providing distance and objectivity between them. As she sums up the point in her essay on 'The Concept of History', what we are left with is

a society of men who, without a common world which would at once relate and separate them, either live in desperate lonely separation or are pressed together into a mass. For a mass-society is nothing more than that kind of organized living which automatically establishes itself among human beings who are still related to one another but have lost the world once common to all of them.[7]

THE HUMAN CONDITION AND THE MODERN AGE

Hannah Arendt suggests, then, that in the modern age men have lost the common world that once made their lives fully human, and have been forced back on to their common nature and their subjective needs and feelings. They are less 'worldly', more 'natural'; and yet even their naturalness is not innocent, for they have become detached from the earth as well. In the last chapter of *The Human Condition* she tries to trace back to its roots in the sixteenth and seventeenth centuries this modern combination of World Alienation and Earth Alienation, and she finds three sources. Firstly, the discovery of America and subsequent exploration of the earth had the paradoxical effect of making the earth seem much smaller, until at last it became possible for modern man to see it as a mere ball from which, first in imagination and then in reality, he could detach himself, viewing it from a point in space. Secondly, the great expropriations of the age of the Reformation started off the process by which all stable property has been devoured by ever-increasing wealth. Thirdly, the invention of the telescope destroyed men's faith in the evidence of their senses. We shall examine in more detail the second and third of these proposed causes of modernity.

According to Hannah Arendt, who follows Marx much of the way on this point, the particularly catastrophic nature of the economic transformation that began in the sixteenth century is due to the fact that it changed stable property into fluid capital. The point of property had always been to provide a settled place in the common world: it was in its nature a stable and durable thing. But the great expropriations since the Reformation period destroyed property without creating it. On the one hand millions of human beings, deprived of their hereditary place in the world, were transformed into mere embodiments of productive labour-power: on the other hand the expropriators treated their acquisitions as capital, the very nature of which is to generate more capital in an endless process. As Marx showed, this process acquires a momentum of its own comparable with a natural process. Within it, production is carried on not for the sake of building a permanent world for human beings to live in, but for the sake of consumption in order to continue the process of production, and for exchange in order to generate more capital and more production. At the same time the 'value' of objects comes to be determined not by their use, beauty or durability—all 'worldly' standards in Hannah Arendt's terms—but by what they will exchange for in the market and what quantity of labour-power has gone into them. According to Hannah Arendt, what has happened has been that the building of a human world has been replaced by an economic process directly analogous to a process of nature; and it seems significant to her that this should have been accompanied by an increasing substitution of sheer labour for skilled work, and have been understood from the first, by economists from Locke to Marx, in terms of the Labour theory of value. For labour is according to her understanding the most natural of men's activities, while work is the most worldly. She quotes Marx as calling labour 'man's metabolism with nature', and suggests that modern economic development, with its substitution of labour for work and of a self-generating process for the building of a world, represents not man's *mastery* over nature, but, on the contrary, the destruction of the world in which such mastery was embodied. All things have become articles of consumption, and with the consequent loss of a stable world and the reduction of work to labour men are reduced to something much closer to nature, a species concerned only with maintaining its life in the endless cycle of production and consumption.

Typical of this development, she thinks, is the fact that labour, which had been despised in all previous civilizations, now rose to a position of unprecedented honour, of which Marx's theories are merely the clearest example. The values of the modern world are labourers' values—life, productivity, abundance—as against the worldly values of work—permanence, stability, durability. The curse of the modern age, then, according to her account, is not that it has become 'unnatural', 'artificial', but that in a significant sense it is not artificial enough. She writes, for example, of automation, the latest stage in this relentless economic process:

The danger of future automation is less the much deplored mechanization and artificialization of natural life than that, its artificiality notwithstanding, all human productivity would be sucked into an enormously intensified life process and would follow automatically, without pain or effort, its ever-recurrent natural cycle. The rhythm of machines would magnify and intensify the natural rhythm of life enormously, but it would not change, only make more deadly, life's chief character with respect to the world, which is to wear down durability.[8]

Furthermore, this modern society of labourers, with its labourers' values of production and consumption and its loss of all other ideals and activities, is threatened, ironically, with the loss of its *raison d'être* as machines make human labourers redundant. In place of the leisure which was for the Greeks the precondition of freedom and action, we have 'the problem of leisure' and the search for hobbies to fill it.

If economic changes have driven man back into his life as a member of his species, Hannah Arendt believes that scientific developments have forced each individual back into his own mind. She dates these changes to the invention of the telescope, the effects of which she believes to have been far reaching. In the first place, by allowing man to penetrate the universe it obliged him to see the earth not as separate from the rest of the cosmos but as part of it, subject to the same laws and by no means its centre: in other words, it enabled man to look at the earth from a universal, cosmic standpoint. This standpoint detached from the earth has made possible the triumphs of modern science over nature; it has also, in the latest developments of contemporary science, enabled man to introduce cosmic processes to the earth—to start off new natural processes hitherto existing only in other parts of the universe, and in doing so to endanger the survival not only of the human world but of the earth itself.

A more immediate result of the invention of the telescope, according to Hannah Arendt, was the reversal of the age-old priority of contemplating over doing. Galileo's instrument demonstrated that merely *contemplating* the heavens in the belief that truth would reveal itself was misguided; on the contrary, nature was deceitful, and could only be trapped into revealing its secrets by human ingenuity, by the invention of clever instruments and experiments. Knowledge comes not through patient observation or rational contemplation, but through doing and making. *Homo faber*, the worker and maker, rose to the position formerly occupied by the philosopher, and knowledge came to be understood in his terms: we know an object when we understand, not what it is or why it is, but *how* it came into being, by what process it became what it is.

The invention of the telescope led to the substitution of a universal for an earthly standpoint and of doing for contemplating in science; in philosophy it led immediately and shatteringly into Cartesian doubt. What the telescope and its confirmation of the Copernican hypothesis demonstrated beyond question was that neither man's unaided senses nor his reason could be trusted to discover truth. Truth, contrary to the age-old assumption, did not reveal itself to the observer, for all human beings since the Creation had been misled by appearances into supposing that the sun moved round the earth. Nothing is certain. Descartes was haunted by the nightmare that 'reality' might be a dream, or that the God who ruled the world might be an evil spirit who deceived man for his own amusement. Philosophers reacted immediately to the shock by retreating to introspection as the only source of certainty. We cannot be certain of the world or anything outside us; but we can at any rate know our own thoughts, our own sensations, the world as it appears in the stream of our consciousness. If we are able to have common knowledge of some things, this is not because we can be sure about the *things* as they stand over against us, but because the common structure of our minds forces certainty upon us. Man can at any rate know what he has made himself, in his own mind.

Initially the pessimism of the philosophers' reaction to the creation of modern science contrasted sharply with the optimism of the scientists themselves, who proceeded enthusiastically to wrest nature's secrets from her in the confidence that what they uncovered was reality. Recently, however, a nightmare akin to Descartes' has begun to haunt them—the fear that the whole structure of scientific knowledge may be only a brilliant human invention, enabling man to manipulate nature, but never allowing him to *understand* anything except the structure of his own thought. Hannah Arendt quotes the suggestion of the eminent physicist Heisenberg [9] that with the ever-increasing sophistication of scientific instruments and techniques, man gets no nearer to observing nature and reality, but instead 'encounters only himself'.

According to Hannah Arendt, the central principle of experimental science, modern philosophy, and historical inquiry alike is that man can only know what he makes himself, with the emphasis heavily on the *process* by which it is made. Initially the general effect of the whole revolution was to raise *Homo faber* and the human capacity for work, for making things, to a new dignity. This is visible in the mechanistic and utilitarian outlook of the early centuries of the modern world, when the craftsman's attitudes and values were dominant. But the emphasis rapidly shifted from producing things to the *process* of production itself, and man the sovereign maker was replaced in modern consciousness by man the labourer within a never-ending, automatic process of production that governs both nature and history. Hannah Arendt suggests that it was the loss of a permanent world, with its

durable objects and standards, and the general retreat from
the common world into introspection, that directed emphasis
away from what is made and replaced it by concentration on
the process of becoming itself. She finds an example of this shift
in the late eighteenth-century translation of the principle of
utility into the Benthamite principle of happiness. Utility is a
throroughly worldly criterion which applies to the objects that
Homo faber makes and the uses for which he makes them. In the
principle of greatest happiness, however, worldly values are
replaced by the subjective sensations of pain and pleasure, and
the only common criterion left is the survival of the species to
which these introspective animals belong.

ON REVOLUTION

As we have seen, a number of interconnected themes run
through Hannah Arendt's analysis of the modern world:
emphasis on the subjectivity of modern man, who is no longer
united with others by a common world: emphasis on the
'naturalness' of modern life, with Life itself, physical cares and
enjoyments and the survival of the species replacing more
specifically human priorities; and emphasis on the way in
which processes have replaced actions and events, so that
modern man experiences himself as engaged in the process of
production, carried along with the process of history and
human evolution, and even as giving habitation to a more or
less automatic 'thought-process' in his own mind. Similar pre-
occupations mark her book *On Revolution*, in which she is again
engaged in trying to understand the modern world, but this
time in the more specifically political terms of revolutions and
revolutionary movements.

Hannah Arendt says in *On Revolution* that 'revolutions are
the only political events which confront us directly and
inevitably with the problem of beginning'.[10] This phenomenon
of a new beginning in the political world, of the creation of
something quite unexpected and marked off from what went
before, strikes her as immensely significant. As we saw in discussing her concept of action, the capacity to start new things
seems to her the human capacity *par excellence* and the manifestation of human freedom; and in this respect her thinking is
consciously directed against some of the most entrenched

assumptions of the modern age. In the seventeenth and eighteenth centuries, in the heyday of the Social Contract theories,
states were commonly thought of as having had a definite
beginning, marked off sharply from a pre-political state by the
deliberate action of men who were often thought of as Founders
or Legislators of more than ordinary human stature. After the
French Revolution, however, this manner of thinking was
challenged and defeated by the new historical consciousness
which is so marked a characteristic of nineteenth-century
culture. It became fashionable to see history as a continuous
stream or process without decisive breaks or beginnings, determined not by the deliberate action of identifiable men but by
Forces which (whether social, economic, intellectual or racial)
were all pictured on the analogy of natural forces. It came to
be taken for granted that apparently decisive actions and
events were in fact only the outward manifestation of long-
term subterranean forces and that, for instance, revolutions
themselves should not be seen as breaks in history, but as parts
of a continuous and necessary process of which the supposed
'actors' were merely tools. This manner of interpreting history
is so much a matter of course by now that it comes as a shock to
find Hannah Arendt insisting upon the possibility of genuine
beginnings, of decisive breaks in history, and of significant
actions by particular men. In this as in some other respects
she has far more in common with the Social Contract theorists
than with intellectual orthodoxy since the early nineteenth
century, and much of her work consists in waging war on the
legacy of nineteenth-century thought.

Revolution, then, represents to her the most striking instance
of the human capacity for beginning new things, for deliberately founding a new political space, which she wishes to
defend against the dehumanizing concepts of automatic processes and irresistible forces which have taken over our thinking
about politics and history. She finds her historical paradigm in
the American Revolution, with its conscious, deliberate action
to found a new Republic that should establish freedom. The
men of the American Revolution, when engaged in their
business of founding the republic, did not feel themselves the
pawns of unintelligible forces that were determining what they
did; they experienced what they were doing as a free, deli-

berate and considered activity, in which the discussions they engaged in and the decisions they came to were of tremendous significance, being decisive for future generations. They were free and responsible, not flotsam upon the stream of history.

However, while the purpose of Hannah Arendt's book is partly to recover and articulate this revolutionary experience of the Founding Fathers, it is also concerned with the fact that the experience has been lost, submerged in the quite different experience of those engaged in the French Revolution, which has determined the revolutionary tradition and affected the course of all revolutions since. The men of the French Revolution began by feeling themselves to be free and responsible actors, but this confidence was rapidly replaced by the terrifying experience, reported by actors and spectators alike, of being caught up in an overwhelming current that deprived them of the possibility of independent action, swept them into positions they would never have deliberately adopted, and finally destroyed them and moved on. The notion of the Revolution as a force in itself, driving forward of its own momentum and carrying along as helpless passengers those who had unwittingly been the instruments of setting it off—this image summed up the experience of the French Revolution, and gave rise to the new nineteenth-century understanding of history as an automatic process over which men have no control. The theme of *On Revolution* is therefore the dialectical contrast between the two revolutions, American and French: the one triumphantly successful, issuing in the foundation of a republic that has stood ever since; the other a disaster, and yet the inspirer of all subsequent revolutionary tradition (which has virtually ignored the American experience): the earlier a vindication of human freedom, the capacity of men to act fearlessly and begin something new; the later a demonstration of human helplessness before the forces which men may set off but cannot keep up with or control. The French Revolution and all subsequent revolutions have been made in the name of freedom, but have notoriously failed to establish it, in the double sense that they have actually established tyranny and have seemed driven by necessity to do so; but the one revolution that *did* establish freedom, the American Revolution, has not only been neglected by the revolutionary tradition but has been reinterpreted by historians in terms of the automatic processes and underlying forces conceived as a result of the experience of the French Revolution.

Hannah Arendt's solution to the riddle is, baldly, that the American Revolution succeeded and established freedom because it was and remained a political revolution, preoccupied with freedom and with forms of government, whereas the French Revolution failed and turned to tyranny because political considerations were rapidly overwhelmed by social ones, by the desire of the masses for liberation from poverty. In eighteenth-century Europe, as in all previous societies, the mass of people were subject to the endless, grinding pressure of necessity, from which only the privileged classes were exempt. America, on the other hand, seemed to all contemporary observers to enjoy an almost miraculous prosperity in that, although there were of course large differences of fortune, even the poor had a sufficiency and were not in misery, not subject to the constant preoccupation with hunger that had always been the lot of most human beings. This fortunate abundance with which the endless new lands of America blessed those who cultivated them had a double effect on the revolutions. On the one hand it meant that, although of course jealousies between rich and poor entered into the political struggles, the men who made the American Revolution could concentrate on political questions of how to generate and distribute power in the new republic without being pressured by a starving mob to legislate for social questions. On the other hand, the knowledge, available in Europe, that misery was not inevitably the lot of mankind, since the Americans had escaped it, gave to the cries of the starving people of Paris a new and urgent tone, and led the French revolutionary leaders to believe that all political considerations should be subordinated to the overwhelming question of how to liberate the masses from hunger. Since nothing that the leaders could do would in fact end this misery the only results were violence, tyranny and revenge, beneath which the original passion for freedom was submerged.

We have already seen, in discussing Hannah Arendt's distinction between freedom and liberation, that a prerequisite of freedom as she understands it is that the man who is to enjoy freedom must first be liberated from subjection to necessity, whether to the tyranny of another man or to the even more exacting tyranny of nature. The man who is constantly hungry, constantly worrying about the next meal for himself and his children, is in no position either to act freely or to appreciate the charms of freedom. His experience of life is entirely in terms of necessity, of being driven by forces outside his control, and when he and a group of others in the same situation begin to move, they do so not with the deliberateness and individual variation of free men but as a solid, united mass pressing with blind force against whatever obstacles they find in their path. According to Hannah Arendt it was the emergence of this mass of the poor on to the public stage in the French Revolution that gave it that character of subordination to necessity that all contemporaries noticed.

Poverty is abject because it puts men under the absolute dictate of their bodies, that is, under the absolute dictate of necessity as all men know it from their most intimate experience and outside all speculations. It was under the rule of this necessity that the multitude rushed to the assistance of the French Revolution, inspired it, drove it onward, and eventually sent it to its doom, for this was the multitude of the poor. When they appeared on the scene of politics, necessity appeared with them, and the result was that the power of the old regime became impotent and the new republic was stillborn; freedom had to be surrendered to necessity, to the urgency of the life process itself.[11]

Her point seems to be that the characteristically human capacity for freedom has only ever been enjoyed by a few men at a time, while the others have been subject to necessity. Since the emergence into the limelight of these masses who had so long lived in obscurity, even action and politics themselves, the proper domain of freedom, have been experienced and interpreted in terms of that necessity which has always been a much more common experience, so that men have all but forgotten that freedom is possible. It was above all Marx who consummated this transformation in theoretical terms, by turning his attention away from the political realm in which men had acted as free agents towards the economic realm where they had always been subject to necessity, and claiming that freedom was an illusion in that the realms of politics and thought were mere superstructures. Hannah Arendt says that he

. . . strengthened more than anybody else the politically most pernicious doctrine of the modern age, namely that life is the highest
good, and that the life process of society is the very center of human
endeavor. Thus the role of revolution was no longer to liberate men
from the oppression of their fellow men, let alone to found freedom,
but to liberate the life process of society from the fetters of scarcity
so that it could swell into a stream of abundance. Not freedom but
abundance became now the aim of revolution.[12]

Marx's theory was ambivalent, however, in that, for all his
compassion for the misery of the poor and his preoccupation
with biological necessity, he retained from his classical education an appreciation of freedom, and hoped, incongruously
enough, that the eventual result of subordinating all political
considerations to the liberation of the poor would be the
foundation of freedom as well. Hannah Arendt claims that
there is a contradiction in his works between the exaltation of
labour as the most characteristic activity of man, and the hope
that labour would eventually become unnecessary or reduced
and that man would emerge from the realm of necessity into
the realm of freedom. Marx 'defines man as an *animal laborans*
and then leads him into a society in which this greatest and
most human power is no longer necessary'.[13] She suggests that
he predicted quite correctly the increasing 'socialization' of
mankind, its ever-increasing preoccupation with the life-
process and its loss of a political realm or an understanding of
freedom, so that politics 'withers away' and all that is left is
'the administration of things': the only flaw in his theory is
that as a result of the contradictions in his thinking he supposed
this to be desirable.[14]

One of Hannah Arendt's objects in *On Revolution*, then, is to
challenge a set of modern assumptions: the general understanding of history in terms of a process, within which men are
instruments rather than actors, and the particular variation on
this theme, most notable in Marxism but widespread in
socialist thinking, which understands revolutions as the
political expression of social upheavals, and sees as their
proper outcome the welfare of the masses. She wishes to
reinstate another, strictly political, understanding of revolution, according to which it is (or can be) a supreme example of
the human ability to act, to create something new and inter-

rupt the blind processes of nature and society. It is noteworthy that her paradigm, the American Revolution, was both a deliberate act of beginning and a 'conservative' action in that it founded a republic and created a constitution. It set up an authority to be preserved and regarded with piety, just as the ancient Romans had felt themselves religiously bound to the foundation of their city. Revolution was not anarchic, but was an act of creation, the addition of a new political realm to the human artifice, something that was meant to be durable and has proved itself to be so. This combination of the *élan* of beginning with the piety of conservation seems to Hannah Arendt to be part of the authentic revolutionary experience which was lost from the French Revolution onwards, to such an extent that revolution and conservation are now thought of not as complementary but as opposites. As she points out, the Americans themselves have now lost the awareness that their own republic was founded by a revolution and have become terrified of any similar attempt by people elsewhere in the world to create a new political realm.[15]

If modern America is not a worthy heir of the true revolutionary spirit, neither, according to Hannah Arendt,[16] is any of the various revolutionary parties and movements that have been so numerous in our century. As we have already seen, she distrusts parties intensely, and regards the socialist and supposedly revolutionary parties as no better than the rest, being authoritarian, preoccupied with social considerations, dominated by ideology and dogged by the belief in historical necessity. Instead she sees as the authentic revolutionaries, and the vindicators of man's power to act and be free, the founders of the abortive revolutionary councils and soviets that have sprung up again and again during revolutions, only to be crushed by party bureaucracies. She notes how Jefferson in his later years worried over the problem of preserving the spirit of the American Revolution against ossification, and proposed as the solution a division of the country into wards small enough to make all citizens constant participators in their government. Just such a system of face-to-face self-government surmounted by federations of the primary units seems to her to have appeared in embryo quite spontaneously in revolution after revolution, foreshadowed by the Paris Commune of the first

French Revolution, conspicuous in its successor of 1871, in the Soviets of the Russian revolutions, the workers' and soldiers' councils in Germany after the First World War, and in the Hungarian Revolution of 1956. What seems striking to her is that, although these cases appear as revivals of the same idea, each case was quite spontaneous, not only unplanned and lacking any conscious tradition but actually contrary to the organization and theoretical tradition of the revolutionary parties. She points out that both Marx in 1871 and Lenin in 1905 reacted originally with enthusiasm to their experience of this spontaneous grass-roots founding of political organs, but later modified their position, since they were committed to a quite different conception of revolution, according to which what happened was that an organized and centralized party seized power from the old government and wielded it. In the Russian case Lenin actually ended by suppressing the Soviets as independent organs when they came into conflict with the party.

Professional revolutionaries as well as conservatives have generally dismissed such attempts to set up popular organs of self-government as obviously impracticable. Hannah Arendt, however, refuses to accept this criticism. A system of popular councils, federated into bodies covering larger areas, seems to her to be a perfectly genuine alternative to rule by parties, and its spontaneous invention in so many separate instances seems to her to indicate the need for some such provision of a public space within which the ordinary citizen can act politically. She emphasizes that the proper function of such councils is political and not administrative: the notion that factories should be run by workers' councils seems to her to indicate a quite false conception of what is involved in economic life and its organization. There, professionalism is entirely appropriate: but it seems to her that in public life the professionalism promoted by party organizations is quite out of place, and that politics should be open to all who choose to engage in it. What she envisages is a system of local councils, the members of which are originally more or less self-selected, since they are composed of those who are willing to take the trouble to interest themselves in public affairs and join with others to form a public space. Within that public space each would be judged by his peers, and those who became, for instance, the deputies in the federation of councils would be those who had earned the trust of their fellow councillors. Since the local councils would remain the units upon which the whole political system was built they would stand in a quite different relation to the federal organs from, for instance, the local councils of Great Britain. Such a system seems to her to be vastly preferable to a party system resting on universal suffrage; and she claims that it would also be practicable, since it has so often sprung into embryonic life, even though it has always so far been strangled at birth.

Much of *On Revolution* is strongly reminiscent of the views of Rosa Luxemburg: the emphasis on the spontaneity of revolution as against theories of historical necessity or professional planning; the exaltation of popular councils as a means of self-government, and the general concern for public freedom. It is clear that Hannah Arendt has much in common with Rosa Luxemburg, and she has written about her with great sympathy.[17] In so far as Hannah Arendt can be said to belong to the Left, it is with republican socialism of the type represented by Rosa Luxemburg that her sympathies lie, and she brings out the great gulf between that and most other forms of socialism, including orthodox Marxism. For Marxism represents for her a summary of most of the dehumanizing tendencies of the modern age, the self-understanding of man as a labourer, producing and consuming instead of acting, the corresponding shift of interest from politics to society, and the belief in historical necessity, sinking human life in an immense process which man cannot alter.

THE CONCEPT OF HISTORY

We have seen Hannah Arendt challenging a whole variety of modern assumptions in her analyses of the modern age—the notion that what is 'natural' is right, the notion that society is the primary reality underlying politics, the belief that direct democracy is impossible, the understanding of revolutions as the outburst of underlying forces instead of the actions of men. Pervading the arguments we have been looking at is a very general challenge to the modern conception of history as a continuous process with an unfolding pattern transcending the stories of the actions of individual men. We shall turn now to her essay on 'The Concept of History', in which she has most fully worked out her study of this conception and her explanation of its origins. Her argument here is particularly intricate, and the summary that follows is a simplified one.

Here again, she makes her point primarily by contrast, by comparing the modern conception of history with that of the ancient Greeks. She points out the close connection between an age's concept of history and its understanding of nature, and relates the Greek concept to their view of nature and the modern to the conception of nature following from the scientific revolution. The essence of the Greek view, as she sees it, is that, to the Greeks, men were the only mortals in an immortal universe. Nature was permanent, moving in endless cycles of growth and decay, eternally repeating itself: man alone existed as a unique individual with a life sharply bounded by birth and death. The aim of men faced with a realization of this situation was to immortalize themselves, to achieve somehow the immortality that belonged naturally to their environment. For the Greek philosophers such immortality was to be found in the contemplation of ultimate reality; but for the earlier Greeks, and notably the poets and historians, a man transcended his mortal existence by the greatness of his deeds, and the purpose of history was to preserve the memory of great deeds so that they were indeed immortal. History therefore consisted of the stories of great men and their great deeds, with the emphasis on individuals in the singular and no conception of their participation in some overall process.

Just as this humanistic Greek concept of history was bound up with the concept of an eternal and inhuman nature, so according to Hannah Arendt the modern concept of history is related to the understanding of nature that emerged out of the scientific revolution of the seventeenth century. And according to her, as we have already seen, the central element in this new attitude to nature was a new activism stemming from distrust of man's senses. Instead of nature simply being there, to be known by contemplation, the new experimental scientists realized that it would yield up its secrets only as a result of men actively experimenting on it, doing things to it, starting processes within it and thus understanding how thing come to be as they are. Man can know only what he has made himself. Vico, who coined this phrase, thought it a sufficient reason to turn from the sciences of nature to the 'New Science' of history; but according to Hannah Arendt, if he had realized the technological potentialities of modern science and the extent to which men now can 'make' nature he would have been a technologist.

Her point is that in the modern age nature is understood in terms of processes and history is understood not as a record of the deeds and sufferings of men worthy to be remembered, but likewise as a process. She stresses how all-pervasive the notion of process is in modern life, in technology, in economics, in our conception of nature and our understanding of history. One of its consequences is that, where everything is understood as being part of a process, and deriving its significance from the process, nothing has meaning in itself. The point of the various stages of a technological process lies in the process as a whole, and in the same way individual human lives and actions are seen as meaningful only in being part of the overall process of history. Where the Greeks would have seen the deeds of, say, Napoleon as significant in themselves, the modern historian instinctively understands them in terms of a general process of which they form a part, as a turning-point, for instance, in the transformation from *Ancien Régime* to modernity all over Europe.

This conception of history as a single continuous process is so familiar that we take it for granted: but Hannah Arendt draws attention to its nature and suggests that it has performed a specific function for those who developed it. She notes that there was an ancient conflict between the Greek notion that man can overcome his mortality by great and memorable deeds in the realm of politics, and the Christian belief that while individual life is eternal this world is ephemeral. During the Christian centuries, it was this eternal life that was emphasized, and the possibility of mortal life being redeemed by earthly greatness was forgotten. At the Renaissance life was secularized again to a large extent, and men were once more regarded as mortals for all practical purposes: but the sense of the redeeming glory of the political realm was not recovered. Instead of the ancient Greek notion that individual greatness, preserved within a political space, could redeem human life from sheer mortality, Hannah Arendt suggests that early modern men developed the notion of the human race as one immortal being, whose endless life, recorded in history as a continuous process, gives mortal individuals a sense of significance. History provides immortality and meaning for human life. Kant, for instance, turned quite explicitly from the apparent meaninglessness of individual events to the overall pattern which could give them significance; Hegel produced a philosophy centred on this kind of universal history, and Marx actually tried to make the conclusion of the historical pattern the deliberate objective of political action.

It seems, however, to Hannah Arendt that this conception of history has encountered precisely the same nemesis as the modern concept of nature. We have already seen that, according to her, modern science rests upon a man-centred conception of nature, not as an eternal, stable environment which can be known by contemplation, but as material for human action to be known by active experiment, transformed by human powers and understood throughout in terms of the category of process, which derives from human actions and their effects (since processes are what is started by human action). But this man-centred conception of nature has disquieting consequences. Hannah Arendt is very much struck by the reflections of the physicist Heisenberg (which she quotes repeatedly) on the limitations of objectivity in science. The point is, crudely, that as scientific theories, techniques and experiments become more and more sophisticated, most of what science discovers is actually human invention. The scientist discovers what will happen in his artificially constructed conditions, and the answers to his highly sophisticated questions: but when he finds, as nuclear physicists have done, that quite different and mutually exclusive theoretical systems can be applied successfully to the same physical events, he may wonder just what it is that science knows. The scientist has learned to *do* things to nature with tremendous success, but the suggestion is that what he *knows* is mainly his own constructions, physical and theoretical. If the enterprise of modern science, originally understood by the scientists as the uncovering of objective reality, in fact leads back to man himself and his capacity for action and invention, the modern concept of history as a continuous process transcending individual life does so too. For the trouble with the notion of appealing from the meaninglessness of individual life to the meaning of history is that too many meanings can be found and the facts will obligingly fall into too many mutually exclusive patterns. Universal histories have been discredited for some time, precisely by the fact that too many different ones can equally well be written; but although contemporary historical speculation is usually on a smaller scale, its thinking is in the same terms.

However, Hannah Arendt's point goes further than this as she pursues her parallel with the scientific investigation of nature. According to her, the weird thing about the situation in science is that although the experiments and the theoretical constructions may all be human inventions, of which any number of variations are possible, men can act successfully in nature on the basis of a great many different possible theories. At the same time that the scientists become doubtful of the truth of their theories, technology triumphantly demonstrates man's power to act on them, whether true or not. It seems to Hannah Arendt more disquieting that something similar is true in the social and political realm: interpretations of history and society, however unfounded, can be made the basis for consistent action, and the action then generates phenomena which support the original ideas. She is thinking here of totalitarianism as she interpreted it: no matter how mad the totalitarian ideology may be, once a whole mass society is marshalled to act in accordance with it it proceeds to prove itself in practice. She sees totalitarianism as an acting out of the realization that 'everything is possible'—that the pattern of human life is not given—and regards this as only the most terrifying aspect of a general loss of *any* given world, uncreated by man, in modern times. Any stable human world has been devoured by economic expansion, and nature itself is being transformed by technology; human society is a field for experiment, and human history, which seemed in the nineteenth century to represent a given overall meaning, now appears as only another invention. As she puts it, echoing Heisenberg,

The modern age, with its growing world-alienation, has led to a situation where man, wherever he goes, encounters only himself.[18]

This is, however, no cause for congratulation, since in order to lead a fully human life man needs a given environment and a stable world for his own life to be set against.

COMMENTS

As must by now be abundantly obvious, Hannah Arendt's theories are highly controversial. Her concepts are formulated precisely to throw into relief the assumptions of modern thought and to challenge them, and her readers are likely to find themselves agreeing or disagreeing vigorously with her contentions. To adjudicate in the controversies she has set on foot is quite beyond the scope of the present book; there are, however, certain aspects of her ideas that do seem to call for some critical remarks because of the striking inconsistencies or ambivalences they contain. One of these is her concept of 'society'.

The problem is that Hannah Arendt's concept of 'society' seems to be a fusion of two separate strands of meaning, the connection between which is not at all clear. The first of these is the analogy she draws between society and the private realm of the Greeks: the household which was the realm of nature and bodily needs, of labour and constraint, contrasted with the public world of the citizens. As we have seen, she suggests that modern society and its economy can be seen as a sort of expansion of this private realm, sharing with it the common concern for biological life. Human life in society, as in the ancient household, consists in a metabolism with nature, not in the vindication of human freedom; and labour, the most natural and constrained of man's capacities, is characteristic of society as it was of the Greek household. This, then, is one strand in Hannah Arendt's concept of society.

The other one, about which we have so far said less (although Hannah Arendt makes frequent references to it) is the notion of society in the sense of high society with its characteristic manners and vices: the fashionable world, originally composed only of a tiny segment of the population, in which appearances were all important, and where the desire to be in fashion and make a good impression led to an ape-like conformity and to the vice of hypocrisy. This high society and its characteristics were most fully observed and recorded in the court life and the salons of the *Ancien Régime* in France; and Hannah Arendt suggests in *On Revolution* [19] that hatred of its corruption and hypocrisy was one of the most violent motives of the French Revolution. She notes in *The Human Condition* [20] how Rousseau, in reacting against the artificiality of this kind of society, tried to vindicate against it a new area of private life, which she calls 'intimacy', in which men could be together with those they genuinely cared about, and emotions and expressions could be sincere. Rousseau and the French revolutionaries felt able to appeal from the hypocritical conformity of fashionable society to the simple, straightforward life and emotions of ordinary people; but according to Hannah Arendt [21] what has happened since their time is that the mores of high society have spread downwards, taking in more and more of the population, until now, in mass societies, no one can escape the universal dominion of appearances, fashion, conformity and hypocrisy.

We have, then, in Hannah Arendt's conception of society, two ill-assorted strands, high society on the one hand and the dominion of nature on the other. We have separated the two for convenience of analysis, but she herself does not do so and moves bewilderingly between them.[22] The two strands have certain things in common, notably the kind of behaviour which both engender: both an overwhelming concern with biological life and a similar concern for appearances give rise to conformity and lack of individual spontaneity: but the differences between the two are much more obvious, and the difficulty of the juxtaposition comes out in Hannah Arendt's curiously ambivalent discussion in *The Human Condition* of 'The Labour Movement'.[23] When reading *The Human Condition* this section strikes one as incongruous, as if it had been introduced after the book was written to paper over a crack in the argument. The problem which it is intended to solve is this. Throughout the book Hannah Arendt has emphasized the connections of labouring with nature, the household and society. She has seen Marx's exaltation of labour as part of the pernicious anti-political growth of society, and has spoken contemptuously of the *animal laborans* and his philistine concern for bodily happiness and nothing else.[24] In contrast to all this, she is nevertheless in the odd position of regarding the labour movement since the nineteenth century as virtually the sole remaining repository of genuine political action and human freedom. She herself poses the problem explicitly [25] and produces an ingenious but unconvincing explanation. She points out that whereas in the ancient world the labourers, who were slaves, were strictly excluded from politics, in the nineteenth century the labouring segment of the population were suddenly admitted to this public realm, 'and this without at the same time being admitted to society, without playing any leading role in the all-important economic activities of this society, and without, therefore, being absorbed by the social realm and, as it were, spirited away from the public'. Consequently the labourers appeared in politics as the opponents of society and all it represented, therefore the only authentically political force. The labouring class has now lost this revolutionary role because it has now been absorbed into society as well, into a mass society that includes everyone.

However, this explanation suffers from the same ambivalence that we have already pointed out as fundamental to Hannah Arendt's whole conception of society. If 'society' is constituted by the emancipation of the labouring process and the loss of all activities except labouring it is hard to see what she can mean by talking about the labouring class being 'admitted to society': while if what she is talking about is 'polite society' and the admission of the labouring class to that, her point becomes the familiar one of the 'bourgeoisification' of the working class, but there is no sign left of her link between society and labour. Her views are further complicated by the fact that whereas in *The Human Condition* she talks about the entrance of the labouring class into politics as a redeeming influence, in *On Revolution*, as we have seen, she suggests that the appearance of the labourers on the public stage in the French Revolution was precisely what brought social considerations and forces into politics. She even suggests there that socialists have been mistaken in supposing that labourers, with their life-long experience of natural necessity, would be likely to understand or value freedom.

When one examines Hannah Arendt's concept of society, therefore, one is left with the impression that in it two separate trains of thought are entangled: that she has plausibly developed both of them, but has not managed to achieve a synthesis between them. The reader may already have noticed in following our summary of her accounts of the modern world that another and deeper ambivalence runs through all of them. In this case the two trains of thought that are not quite integrated concern man's power in the modern age, and his powerlessness; the ambivalence between them crops up in many forms in Hannah Arendt's writings. One of its forms concerns man's relation to nature. On the one hand, she describes modern man as worldless: she notes and deplores the loss by man in modern times of the human artifice, the man-made world of objects that stood between man and nature. This gives us the impression that modern man is more in accord with and exposed to nature than he used to be or should be. On the other hand, she also points out that in modern times more and more of our environment is man-made—even nature itself, as technology reaches unprecedented heights. We have seen her (particularly in her essay on 'The Concept of History') deploring the fact that there is now nothing that is *not* man-made and artificial: nothing is given any more. Both points surely contain truth about our situation, and they are not precisely contradictory; but they stand in an uneasy relation to one another that is nowhere explicitly worked out.

A similar contrast between power and powerlessness is to be found in her account of totalitarianism. There she provides us with two opposed pictures of the totalitarian leaders. On the one hand, as we have seen, she describes them as following their ideology and participating in the processes of nature or history as though they were automatons, not free men. On the other hand she talks of their belief that everything is possible, and their cynicism about even their own ideologies, giving an impression of complete arbitrariness that, in its power to start things, ought surely to be seen as an example of action in her own sense.

Again the same ambivalence occurs with regard to the general question of the capacity of modern men for action. As we have seen, Hannah Arendt constantly deplores the apparent loss of the capacity to act in modern times, and stresses that modern men no longer act, but only participate in processes and behave in a conformist manner.[26] On the other hand, she says in 'The Concept of History'[27] that the main characteristic of modern man is precisely action. True, she is talking there of science and technology, of the modern habit of 'acting into nature' and starting processes in nature; but she also says some interesting things there about the notion of process. We have seen her stigmatizing behaviour and participation in processes as the opposite of action; but here she says that processes are what is started by human action, and that the reason why the category of process dominates the modern age is that it is a corollary of the dominance of action. By understanding nature and, later, history and society in terms of processes we are thinking anthropomorphically, projecting our experience of the outcome of human actions on to things outside us. Men are enmeshed in processes; but processes follow from human action. Here again, we have the ambivalence about whether man's power is increased or diminished. Here again, both sides of the question ring true, and are not exactly inconsistent, but there is no explicit articulation of the relation between them.

What is interesting about these ambivalences is that Hannah Arendt appears in each case to have followed two different lines of thought simultaneously, working out each of them, bringing them close to one another, but not actually clarifying their relationship. This tells us much about her manner of thinking, which is unusually multidimensional. Where many thinkers proceed by working out one line of argument at a time, Hannah Arendt characteristically has a great many linked trains of thought in her mind at once. This makes her writings both rich and complex: often, as in the case of the essay on 'The Concept of History', one is left with the sense of a mind striving with immense effort to unravel and articulate a tremendously complex set of insights, so that their clear statement on paper is a considerable achievement, and it is not surprising if some loose ends remain to be tied up.

5
Politics and Thought

In the first chapter of this book we stated that Hannah Arendt had a particular and unusual understanding of the business of politics and of the business of thinking, and that she propounded these in conscious opposition both to contemporary social science and to the great tradition of political theory. It will, we hope, be fairly clear by now what her position is, but in this final chapter we shall be concerned firstly to clarify and sum up her conception of the political and her linked views on thinking and the pursuit of truth and secondly to consider her differences from other schools of political thought and whether or not her thinking is in fact truer to the reality of politics than theirs.

Our first concern, then, is with her understanding of the political and of thought itself, and we can find an illuminating expression of this in one of her essays, 'The Crisis in Culture: Its Social and Its Political Significance'.[1] One respect in which Hannah Arendt differs conspicuously from most contemporary schools of political study is her fondness for the essay form as a means of expression. The freedom of the essay suits admirably her manner of discursive reflection, exploring the implications of a subject into unlooked-for ramifications. In the essay with which we are at present concerned there is a discussion of Kant's *Critique of Judgment* [2] that will help us to pin down more closely her understanding of the political; and it is characteristic of her that a discussion of the classic of aesthetics should provide her with an opportunity to explore the nature of politics.

Hannah Arendt maintains that the *Critique of Judgment* contains a profound understanding of politics, and is much more relevant than the *Critique of Practical Reason*, which has been more commonly cited as a source of Kant's political thought. The latter is dominated by the categorical imperative, 'always act in such a manner that the principle of your action can become a general law'; and Hannah Arendt points out that this derives its force from the notion of consistency, of agreeing with oneself, that is essential to rational thought. It is geared to thought rather than to action, to the individual rather than the group of men. But the kind of thinking that Kant describes in the *Critique of Judgment* consists, he says, of an 'enlarged mentality', able to 'think in the place of everybody else'. Counter to the common assumption that aesthetic judgment is a 'matter of taste' and merely private, Kant maintains that it is an essentially public function, for two reasons. In the first place, a judgment is not simply an ejaculation, but seeks to commend itself to the agreement of others: implicitly or explicitly it seeks public recognition. And in the second place, judgment sound enough to obtain such agreement cannot be achieved in isolation: the judging person must, if only in imagination, have others and their perspectives present to him if he is to judge properly. In fact, judgment as described by Kant strikes Hannah Arendt as being a peculiarly *political* capacity because it involves thinking (actually or in imagination) in the presence of others, considering their viewpoints as well as one's own and seeking their acceptance of one's judgment. In being so intrinsically related to others, to our sharing of the world, and to the common sense that belongs to that common world, it is quite different from philosophical thinking, which Hannah Arendt sees as the essentially single-minded pursuit of truth, within one mind and outside and beyond the world of common sense. Philosophy has always looked for truth that would be absolute, and has tended to condemn judgments, for instance of taste, as merely subjective and arbitrary. But Kant insists, and Hannah Arendt reiterates, that taste, though not absolute, is not arbitrary either. It is not a matter of private feeling, but of feeling in which others are expected to concur: that is to say it is concerned with the world common to men. Although each sees this world from a slightly different standpoint, sound judgments are nevertheless not limited by this standpoint but take account also of the positions of others and can therefore be shared by them. Similarly Hannah Arendt notes that although judgments of taste do not compel assent as logical demonstrations do, they can be not merely arbitrary, but persuasive. It seems to her that in this they resemble political modes of intercourse, which differ from tyranny in being based on persuasion instead of coercion.

Hannah Arendt's seizing on Kant's account of judgment as a description of a political capacity is typical of her mode of inventive reflection, and it also brings out much of the quality of her conception of the political. What becomes particularly clear is the *spatial* quality of politics: in politics, as in judgment, any acting or thinking person is in the presence of others, not withdrawn into himself but surrounded by many other distinct individuals—each one himself capable of acting and thinking, each one commanding a particular view of the common world—among whom he must move and with whom he must come to terms. This spatial imagery expresses Hannah Arendt's sense of human diversity and plurality, the fact, as she puts it,[3] that 'not one man, but men, inhabit the earth'. This is not merely a matter of diverse interests: interests, after all, are characteristically shared by groups or classes of people. It is a matter of the ability of every individual to act, to begin things, to be unpredictable. Politics, to Hannah Arendt, is the fruitful coexistence of these unique ever-new individuals. But the difficulties of such coexistence seem to her to entail the constant danger of non-political solutions that simplify the teeming richness of human life and thereby destroy freedom.

The most obvious of these solutions is of course tyranny. The tyrant imposes his rule by violence and crushes resistance, leaving a situation in which only *his* individuality, *his* capacity for originating projects, *his* thoughts and *his* standpoint can be taken notice of, while his subjects are reduced to an inert and less than human condition. Totalitarianism, according to Hannah Arendt, goes even further than plain tyranny in destroying human plurality, since besides the systematic terror eliminating almost all human capacities on the part of its victims, the whole population is enlisted in a movement where each is only a servant of and expression of an ideology, and personal actions are replaced by the working out of the ideology, personal thoughts by its standpoint.

It is obvious enough that Hannah Arendt's conception of

politics must be utterly opposed to tyranny and totalitarianism. What is more interesting from our point of view is that this conception of politics goes with a particular attitude to thinking, and with a distrust of the traditional quest of philosophy and science for truth. In the same essay to which we have already referred she goes on from her suggestion that there are affinities between aesthetic taste and the world of politics to discuss the possible opposition between political judgment and the absolutes of the artist and the philosopher.[4] She quotes with approval Cicero's remark that he would rather err in the company of Plato than be right with Plato's opponents, and she interprets this statement as the expression of a truly political mind, one to whom freedom is of such central importance that he will not be coerced even by the truth. And in fact one of the constantly recurring themes of her writings is this opposition between the claims of truth and the claims of humanity.

In order to throw into relief the highly individual nature of her position, let us consider for a moment the values to which even the 'value-free' social scientists of our time are committed. When Max Weber developed the notion of value-freedom [5] his object was to exclude from social science the various political biases of the social scientist himself and of those who were in a position to influence him : but he took for granted that for the purposes of science a commitment to truth regardless of consequences was essential. That he was himself aware of the tension between the demands of science and the demands of politics is clear from the two parallel essays in which he described 'Science as a Vocation' and 'Politics as a Vocation'; however, his 'value-free' successors in political science have followed him in assuming, usually without argument, that a commitment to truth is the one 'value' their calling allows them. This commitment to truth before all else, however appropriate to science and philosophy, seems to Hannah Arendt to be misplaced where politics and political thinking are concerned, for she would rather place as the supreme value to which all else must give way not truth but freedom. She is not offering a recommendation of propagandist lying, but making the point that the quest for truth as the supreme value is not at all necessarily compatible with freedom.

Truth, she says, is essentially coercive: it is in its nature to silence opinion and impose uniformity. This is partly because those who believe themselves to possess the truth will always be disinclined to tolerate error—the schemes of some liberals for spreading enlightenment have been surprisingly authoritarian [6]—but Hannah Arendt has in mind more than this common human failing. She is thinking partly of the rigid, coercive nature of that paradigm of truth for so much of Western thought, the logical argument. Deductive reasoning, where everything follows once you admit the first premise, allows no escape within the limits of merely logical thinking: there is no way out of the tramlines of argument, however much common sense may cry out against its conclusion. This suspicion of deductive logic (which seems to her to have essential affinities with dogmatism and ideology) pervades her thought. More fundamentally, however, the whole notion of absolute truth, the truth of a system or a doctrine, seems to her to be a threat to the freedom characteristically embodied in the life of politics simply because it allows no room for human diversity.

She has expressed these ideas most clearly in an essay on Lessing, a writer with whom she has great sympathy.[7] Lessing's play, *Nathan der Weise*, is concerned with the conflict between truth (in the shape of religious doctrine) and friendship, and gives priority to the latter. Unlike most thinkers, Lessing consciously preferred the uncertainty of opinion to the wished-for certainty of truth, and was glad that none of the claims to truth so far advanced in favour of any doctrine was unchallengeable. His feeling was that absolutely unquestionable knowledge of the truth would have cut short that free play of opinion and discussion in which fully human existence is carried on. In Lessing's time it was chiefly in terms of religion that the question of truth versus opinion arose, whereas Hannah Arendt remarks that in our time it is science that is the home of the absolute to which it is a sacred duty to sacrifice friendship and humanity. Clearly in saying this she is thinking above all of the devotion of party members to those pseudo-scientific ideologies in the names of which millions have been murdered, and their willingness to betray their friends and relations for the sake of what they believed to be the truth; but her point applies also to the quest for truth inherent in science. Were the dream of science, of a fully proven body of knowledge on every subject, to be realized, this would detract from human life since there would be no longer any room for diversity of opinion. As we shall see, however, Hannah Arendt believes that the sphere of opinion deserves more study and discrimination than it usually receives. Like Lessing, she is repelled by the inevitable uniformity of truth, and attracted by the constant dialectical struggle of opinions against one another. She points out that Lessing used to choose his polemical positions not on grounds of the truth of the doctrine he supported at any particular time, but for the thoroughly political reason that one particular school appeared to stand in need of assistance at one time, another at another. This of course made him appear inconsistent (as those who pursue policies in international relations based on the principle of the balance of power seem inconsistent to those who view policies in ideological terms). But he was not concerned with consistency: his aim was less to solve the problems that thought poses—for such solution would put an end to thought—than to stimulate thought in others and thereby bring about discussion. Here, the very image of thought is spatial, not at all the withdrawn internal dialogue of the philosopher with himself but the endless conversation of friends in the marketplace.

It should not be thought that either Lessing or Hannah Arendt is an admirer of sheer arbitrariness, of views adopted without thought and expressed without responsibility. On the contrary, the diversity of opinion seems to Hannah Arendt a function of its being the genuine product of thought. She quotes with evident approval a striking passage from the *Federalist Papers* to the effect that when men exert their reason upon any subject, they fall naturally into different opinions, whereas when they are governed by a common passion they are unanimous—a resounding challenge to the tradition that reason speaks to men with one voice. In *On Revolution* Hannah Arendt develops her conception of opinion and states that it should not be bracketed with interest, from which it differs completely.[8] Interests enter politics as the possession of groups, but opinions are formed by and belong to individuals, and cannot belong to groups unless by all but one aping the genuine opinion of another. Where a so-called 'public opinion' exists and all the people seem to speak with one voice, what has in fact happened is that real opinion has ceased to exist at all, for in order to form his own opinion, each individual requires the surrounding environment of the multitude of other opinions.

Where unanimity exists, in other words, some form of coercion is at work, whether it be the coercion of a tyrant, the coercion of interest or passion, or the coercion of logic that makes us admit the logical conclusion of an argument. When men are free, their opinions are different because they themselves are distinct individuals and have different standpoints from which to view the world. This is not to say, however, that their opinions may not be more or less valid in being more or less comprehensive. In an essay on 'Truth and Politics'[9] Hannah Arendt has remarked that political thinking is 'representative', in that it involves forming opinions and arriving at judgments by first representing to oneself the points of view of as many others as possible, and comprehending them, as the condition of arriving at a conclusion. This kind of thinking reaches validity not by means of conclusive proof but by running all round its object in order to see it in many different perspectives; it can therefore never be self-evident, but it can be far from arbitrary. An opinion so arrived at, in so far as it is valid generally, is so by virtue of respecting and comprehending the diversity of men and their standpoints.

That is to say, opinion is both inescapably individual and intrinsically linked to the common world which each individual shares with others: it differs from the search for truth not only in being more personal but also in being more public, not divorced from the common life as philosophy and science have always tended to be. By a curious irony it is the seeker after absolute truth, which would compel the assent of all, who has no need to consider the viewpoints of other men, and has indeed often lived withdrawn from them. But however justifiable or necessary such an attitude may be in philosophy or in science, in politics, the realm *par excellence* of human diversity and multiplicity, it must be utterly out of place. To Hannah Arendt, political thinking belongs honourably within the sphere of opinion, and attempts to fit it to the pursuit of truth can only injure it.

So far we have given the impression that truth is not a very high priority to Hannah Arendt, and certainly where the scientific ideal of general truths is concerned that is the case. However, there is another aspect of truth that does gravely concern her, and this concern is entirely characteristic, for it is with truth in the particular, not in the general: with the true story of the events that are the stuff of politics. It is not so much scientific, philosophical or religious truth, but simple, single, contingent fact that strikes Hannah Arendt as both very fragile and absolutely indispensable to human life. She has explored the subject in her essay on 'Truth and Politics'. She distinguishes in the traditional manner between rational truth and factual truth, and explains that it was rational truth that first came into conflict with politics, when Plato and his successors opposed philosophy to opinion, the stuff of politics, as the life of the philosopher was opposed to the life of the citizen. This particular conflict is no longer with us, but there is in our day a greater conflict between factual truth and politics than ever before. The most conspicuous examples of this occur in totalitarian rewriting of history so that, for instance, Trotsky ceases to have existed or played any part in the Russian revolution; but Hannah Arendt maintains that there is an equally disturbing tendency in freer countries for the line between fact and opinion to be blurred, and for facts that are unwelcome to particular political groups to be treated as if they were opinions to be discussed, not truths that must be accepted.

Reflecting on this situation, she points out, as we have seen, that truth of all kinds, including factual truth, is essentially coercive, demanding acceptance, and is therefore a power that is liable to come into conflict with political power or to be irksome to the freedom of citizens. But while all truth, in being domineering in this way, goes against the grain of political life, factual truths have the peculiar weakness of being completely contingent. Facts have no self-evidence or rational consistency to recommend them; they are no more self-evident than opinions, and can be established only by evidence and testimony, the various links in which are always fallible. Facts are therefore very easy to destroy. Organized lying can wipe out all memory of what happened, and once lost it can never be recovered. When such lying is destroying the truth, the man who attempts to preserve it and tell what really happened suffers from the disadvantage that, since facts are hopelessly contingent, what really happened may quite well sound less likely and less persuasive than the lie that is being put in its place. If it were only a matter of occasional spasmodic lying, the surrounding context of truth would show up the lies and make them less harmful: but in the modern phenomena of rewriting history and creating images, political and commercial, lying is undertaken on such a large scale that it is very hard to distinguish from reality. One consequence is that when, as inevitably happens, changes in power relations ordain changes in the system and consequently a new set of lies, the end result among the whole population is a condition of total cynicism in which no criteria for distinguishing between truth and lies, reality and fiction remain. In other words, according to Hannah Arendt, where politics destroys factual truth it also destroys the common world shared by everyone which is the necessary space in which political action can be carried on.

In this essay, Hannah Arendt presents factual truth as standing in an ambiguous relation to politics: in tension with the political world of free action, opinion and persuasion, but at the same time recording political events and contributing to the common world within which events can take place. Facts are stubborn and unyielding, but they are also a witness to human freedom in that they record the contingent, unsystematic, non-deducible way in which men acted and things happened. Her view of the relation of truth to politics therefore has two elements: on the one hand a respect and concern for the facts which provide the true record of men's actions; on the other a wish to defend opinion—in its richness and diversity a truly political mode of thought—against philosophical or scientific attempts to replace it by some systematic truth.

Hannah Arendt only rarely mentions or argues explicitly with the views of the social scientists who now form the orthodoxy of political study, but it is obvious that her thinking stands implicitly in opposition to theirs and is intended as a challenge to it. Let us therefore attempt to sum up the broad ways in which she differs from the social scientists (her differences from all who would call themselves by that name are too wide for it to be fruitful to differentiate for this purpose among the various schools of social or political science). Clearly, her whole conception of politics differs from theirs. In the first place, as we have seen, she is opposed to all modes of thought that comprehend politics within society and explain what is taken to be the part in terms of the whole. Against all accounts of politics in terms of social class, stage of social development, social structure and function she asserts the autonomy of politics. She is prepared to agree, as we have seen, that to a large extent in modern times politics *has* been merely an offshoot of society, but that she takes to be a peculiarity of the period rather than part of the order of nature. No doubt she would not deny social explanations of politics a limited validity and usefulness, but her point is to direct attention back from society to the acting individuals who carry on political life. Similarly with any understanding of politics in terms of the overall system, structure or roles: she counters all such modes of thinking by the heavy emphasis she lays upon the particular actions and interactions within any system, and the freedom of the unique individuals who occupy the roles.

Again, as we have seen, her emphasis on man the acting individual is directed against social scientists' interest in man the behaving member of a mass. The whole notion of studying politics by gathering statistics of mass behaviour and mass 'opinion' seems to her misguided because it is bound to catch only the predictable routine behaviour and reactions, while missing precisely the unique actions and thoughts that make history. Since these actions and thoughts are in the nature of things much rarer than mass behaviour they will never look statistically significant. Consequently by placing their emphasis on statistics the social scientists are consciously or unconsciously defining man as a behaving animal, and by doing so ruling out the possibility of unique, unpredictable action. Conceiving man in this way, they fall naturally into a determinist view of politics and history, seeing them as a pattern of processes that ought in principle to be predictable if we had enough information. Hannah Arendt's conception of freedom is asserted vigorously against just this belief in necessity and predictability, and the futurologists come in for her most explicit condemnation. In her essay *On Violence* [10] she attacks futurology on the grounds that its predictions are nothing but projections of processes that are in train now, and will continue if, but only if, men do not act and thereby alter them.

Events, by definition, are occurrences that interrupt routine processes and routine procedures; only in a world in which nothing of importance ever happens could the futurologists' dream come true.

Any attempt to account for unpredictable actions and events by labelling them 'random happenings' is, she suggests, simply a device to protect the futurologists' view of the world against the things that constantly disprove it.

One may perhaps sum up the differences between Hannah Arendt's views and those of the social scientists by saying that she objects to their whole attempt to offer *general* explanations in politics (on the model of the general laws of physics and other sciences) and in doing so to ignore or detract from the specific, particular, unique course of events and the actors who make it. This objection to the desire for generality that blurs vision of the specific comes out also when she accuses social scientists of imprecise use of language and the inability to make distinctions.[11] She notes, for example, a tendency to lump together authoritarian government, tyranny and totalitarianism without distinguishing amongst them, and she suggests that one reason for this kind of lapse is the functionalization of concepts: the specific differences between one form of government and another, one kind of religion and another, even between religion and politics, are ignored on the assumption that all societies involve a certain range of basic functions, and that whatever fulfils the same function in any society is *really* the same thing. This is yet another case in which, according to Hannah Arendt, the rich diversity of human life is simplified for the sake of achieving a supposedly true system of thought.

This brings us to the differences between Hannah Arendt's conception of political thinking and that prevalent among social scientists. Here, as we have seen, the crucial point is that where most of her contemporaries see political study as a matter of science, aiming at proven truth, Hannah Arendt sees it as a matter of opinion, aiming at validity but in a different way. This has important consequences. Because the social scientist aims at truth that will be demonstrable and settled, he is inevitably led to choose his subject-matter and the focus of his work less on the basis of its intrinsic interest than because it is amenable to investigation by reliable scientific methods such as the collection of statistics. Hence the many pieces of research revealing nothing more interesting than the responses of anonymous persons to somewhat vacuous questionnaires. Hannah Arendt, on the other hand, since she is consciously engaged in thinking that belongs to the genre of opinion rather than science, can go directly to questions of real interest and significance.[12] Naturally, what she has to say has none of the demonstrable, unchallengeable assurance of truth at which science aims, but then that is not her object. Throughout her work her emphasis is on human diversity, on the richness, complexity and unpredictability of human life, and her writing is not only a celebration of the personal and unique but also an example of it—the creation of a personal point of view from which many things become visible, which can be shared with others but which remains her own. In her introduction to the essays collected in *Beyond Past and Future* [13] she is careful to emphasize that her essays are 'exercises in how to think'—not final solutions nor parts of a system. Her thought is personal, belonging to no one else and claiming no absolute validity; it is at the same time public, in being formed in constant dialogue with that of others and in commending itself to our acceptance. The disadvantage of her approach is of course that her lines of thought at times become personal to the point of seeming merely arbitrary. However, this limited appeal of her thought could not seem to her to be a decisive disadvantage, since she does not subscribe to the scientific ideal of a system which, being proved true, all must accept. Her aim is rather, in the constant interchange of separate thinking minds, to add something to the discussion and to provoke new thought on the part of some at least of these minds. In this aim there is surely no doubt that she succeeds.

The modern writers on politics with whom Hannah Arendt has most in common are those who also write in a highly personal and idiosyncratic manner, such thinkers as, for instance, Eric Voegelin, Simone Weil, Bertrand de Jouvenel or Michael Oakeshott.[14] What all this heterogeneous collection have in common is their individual, reflective manner of approach to politics, their ability to write well, and perhaps a common opposition to academic orthodoxy; but they certainly cannot be said to form a school in any sense, and would all disagree with one another. Perhaps, however, one can say that they would disagree respectfully: it is noteworthy, for instance, that in Hannah Arendt's exchange with Voegelin,[15] although their views are quite different, she clearly has considerable respect for him as a thinker.

In our introductory chapter we saw that Hannah Arendt's aim has been to do justice to the reality of political experience in a way that neither political science nor the great tradition of political theory has done; we must therefore turn now to the question whether or not she has succeeded in this endeavour. Is her own political thinking truer to politics than the views she opposes? We can perhaps approach this question indirectly, via a comparison of her views with those of another recent defender of politics, Professor Bernard Crick. Professor Crick, in his book *In Defence of Politics*,[16] has spiritedly defended it against many of the dangers by which Hannah Arendt sees it threatened, notably against social science and doctrinaire ideology. Like Hannah Arendt he distrusts all attempts to replace human diversity by the uniformity of a system, a science or a leader, and he is, like her, a great quoter of *The Federalist Papers* on the inevitability of diverse opinions and interests in any state, and the need for a political structure that can accept this diversity. Like Hannah Arendt, he regards politics as a positively worthwhile activity, not an unfortunate necessity. The similarities between the two writers are quite striking (and indeed Professor Crick remarks in the Preface to his revised edition of *In Defence of Politics* that he has realized since writing it that he is indebted to Hannah Arendt). However, the differences between them are no less striking. These can be expressed succinctly by saying that where Hannah Arendt's political thinking is romantic, Crick's is matter of fact. When Crick talks about politics, defends it against its enemies and sings its praises, what he has in mind is British (and to a lesser extent American) party politics as it actually exists, warts and all, including the manœuvring, the compromises, the tactical changes of position and the intra-party struggles for power. Hannah Arendt, on the other hand, makes it clear that ordinary party politics does not count as real politics within her conception of it. What she has in mind is chiefly a glorified Greece and Rome, plus the occasional moments of revolution when real political action has briefly revisited the modern world. Crick's conception of politics is one that is firmly ensconced in English political tradition and practice, whereas Hannah Arendt's is alienated from the world of actual affairs. In keeping with this fundamental difference are others. Where Hannah Arendt sees politics in terms of single individuals, their diversity and their unique capacity for action, Crick sees it rather in terms of the plurality of groups and interests within a community; and his praise of tolerance and compromise is a matter of preferring a peaceful and non-oppressive solution to these clashes of interest, not of gaining glory to redeem the futility of human life. Since he also places a high value on order it seems unlikely that he would sympathize with the more anarchic aspects of Hannah Arendt's much more romantic conception.

It may be suggested, therefore, that whereas Crick's conception of politics is quite close to real politics as it is actually carried on in this and other countries, Hannah Arendt's is a romantic dream that is as far from reality as any of the conceptions she opposes, if in a different direction. Certainly her conception of politics as exemplified by the Greek *polis* and by workers' councils seems rather an extravagant one. As we have seen, she contrasts such situations, in which individual men and women are engaged in redeeming their existence by stepping forward from their private lives into the light of the public realm, with the murky world of parties, their petty caballing, careerism and dogmatism. However, all these vices of the party spirit certainly existed in abundance in the ancient Greek city-state, while it is hard to imagine that, had the various revolutionary councils she extols lasted a little longer, there would have been no similar growth of cabals intriguing against one another, sects trying to put one another down, and self-seeking individuals aiming at dominance. A look at comparable semi-political units like popular pressure groups, voluntary associations and so on would surely be illuminating in this respect: for although some men and women certainly find a place in such bodies for action in Hannah Arendt's sense, with all its virtues, many others involve themselves for less praiseworthy reasons and behave in less admirable ways. It is not quite so obvious as she seems to think that it would be better to have a country run by the sort of people who run voluntary organizations than by careerist politicians. Hannah Arendt appears, in fact, to have fallen into the familiar trap of romanticizing The People. She does actually say [17] that those who distrust the people are mistaking for it what is actually the mass—but since she provides us with no means of telling the one from the other, this does not help much.

Hannah Arendt's romanticized model of true politics is undoubtedly open to objection, and certainly does not seem very close to political experience. Nevertheless her ideas *do* illuminate the understanding of politics in more general ways. This will, we hope, already have become clear in the course of this book; but let us briefly consider some of the ways in which her ideas do indeed focus attention on aspects of political experience that are neglected both within the tradition of political theory and in contemporary political science.

The central point of her thinking is her insistence that men are unique individuals capable of original action. No one in the great tradition of political thought has brought home this truth, while the prevailing trends of social and political thought today are quite opposed to it. The great strength of most contemporary political study lies in its revelation of the importance of such generalities as system, structure, class and role; and to think in such terms is undoubtedly illuminating. However, it presupposes a particular view of the human condition (indeed, one of Hannah Arendt's merits is to force upon social scientists who would prefer to avoid philosophical pretensions the realization that their views do presuppose a working conception of the human condition) and like all such views this is partial, distorting as well as illuminating. Where system, structure, class and role are emphasized, and human individuality and action correspondingly neglected, the natural trend is to a deterministic picture of life within which events ought in principle to be predictable and forces calculable. It ought, for instance, to be possible to describe and classify all the social forces and structural weaknesses that produce revolutions, or to calculate the relative power of states in such a way as to be able to predict the outcome of a war between given contenders. And yet political events constantly stagger the onlooker by their unpredictability. By what means, given any amount of information, could anyone have predicted, for instance, the transformation of China, for so long the paradigm of conservatism, into a revolutionary society of enormous energy? Or even that revolutionary China would be admitted to the United Nations? It is a continual experience in politics that analyses of situations that seem at the time to be exhaustive and to consider all possible outcomes are rapidly put out of date by contingencies that would have seemed impossible only a short time before. Apparently insoluble conflicts suddenly turn out to be capable of compromise; quite new situations and problems are created. The constant contingency of politics baffles systematic description; and it is this aspect of political experience that Hannah Arendt does illuminate by her emphasis on the constant power of each individual man to act in ways that no one could predict, to create new systems and roles and shatter those he inherits, to begin new processes that can be told as intelligible stories only after the event. Like all political theories, hers too is lopsided: for the sake of emphasis she lays tremendous stress on the anarchic and creative capacities of human beings and pays little attention to their life as conforming members of structures. However, she is surely justified in over-emphasizing what the trends of our time might incline us to forget altogether.

Our answer to the question, does Hannah Arendt succeed in illuminating political experience, is therefore twofold. Her ideal model of what politics should be is surely too romantic to be helpful: but her general conception of the human condition really does help us to see aspects of politics that tend to be unjustifiably neglected. That is to say, she is most illuminating when she talks about the human condition in general, least so when she apparently gets down to brass tacks and discusses the virtues of councils as opposed to parties.

This is not as surprising as it may seem. When we consider the great writers of the tradition of political thought we find that it is their general reflections that give them their claim to greatness, not the acuteness of their judgments on the politics of their day nor the wisdom of their particular recommendations. This is of course partly because times have changed and we are no longer particularly interested in what Plato thought about the Cretan state or Burke about French finance. But apart from this effect of time, which winnows away the particular and leaves the general, it is also the case that a writer's particular judgments and recommendations are often more parochial, more limited by his own experiences and prejudices than his more general reflections. Burke is an obvious case in point. His judgments on the French Revolution are extremely one sided, his picture of the *Ancien Régime* much romanticized and his recommendations eventually fanatical—but nevertheless his political thought remains immensely illuminating at the general level because of the truth of much of his picture of the human condition. The same applies to most of the great figures in the history of political thought: whatever we may think of their particular political judgments and their personal political ideals (consider those of Hobbes, for instance) they continue to illuminate politics now by virtue of what they tell us about the human condition, each emphasizing some aspect of it that others had neglected.

We saw in the first chapter of this book that Hannah Arendt criticized the whole tradition of political thinking for being in a sense *un*political, neglecting the experience of men of action for the outlook of the philosopher. Certainly it is true that her own picture of politics is unlike any other in the tradition in the emphasis that it lays on action as a human capacity. Nevertheless Hannah Arendt belongs also to that same tradition by virtue of the generality of her thinking: what she has to say about politics, and her power to shed light upon it, are contained in her understanding of the human condition.

Notes

The pages cited in the works by Hannah Arendt refer to the American editions, as listed in the Bibliography.

CHAPTER ONE

1. *The Human Condition*, p. 5.
2. *Ibid.*, pp. 150–2.
3. *The Origins of Totalitarianism*, pp. 470–3.
4. pp. vii–viii.
5. 1960.
6. *Between Past and Future*, p. 146.
7. 'Peace or Armistice in the Near East', *Review of Politics*, Vol. 12, No. 1, Jan. 1950.
8. *The Methodology of the Social Sciences*, ed. Shils and Finch, Free Press, New York, 1949, particularly pp. 21, 53–4.
9. *Between Past and Future*, p. 6.
10. *Ibid.*, p. 165.
11. See for instance her remarks on Hobbes, *The Origins of Totalitarianism*, p. 139 *et seq.*
12. See 'Epilogue: Reflections on the Hungarian Revolution', added to the second (1958) edition of *The Origins of Totalitarianism*.

CHAPTER TWO

1. *The Origins of Totalitarianism*, third edition, 1966, p. 460.
2. *Ibid.*, p: 382.
3. *Ibid.*, p. 433.
4. *Ibid.*, p. 438.
5. *Ibid.*, p. 475.
6. *Review of Politics*, Vol. 15, Jan. 1953, pp. 76–85.
7. *The Origins of Totalitarianism*, p. 459.
8. 'The Phantom World of the Dark Continent', *The Origins of Totalitarianism*, p. 186.
9. *The Origins of Totalitarianism*, p. 227.
10. *Ibid.*, p. 401.

11. *Ibid.*, p. 318.
12. *Ibid.*, e.g. p. 460.
13. *Ibid.*, pp. 458–9.
14. *Ibid.*, p. xi.
15. *Ibid.*, p. ix.
16. *The Burden of Our Time*, 1951, pp. 429–30.
17. e.g. p. 188 re gold and superfluousness.
18. *loc. cit.*, p. 78.
19. *The New Science of Politics*, University of Chicago Press, Phoenix edition, 1966, Chapter VI, 'The End of Modernity'.
20. *The Origins of Totalitarianism*, p. 353.
21. An adequate discussion of the validity of Hannah Arendt's account would involve wide methodological issues which are unfortunately beyond the scope of this book.
22. *The Origins of Totalitarianism*, pp. 79–88.

CHAPTER THREE

1. 'A Reply' to Eric Voegelin's Review of *The Origins of Totalitarianism*, *Review of Politics*, Vol. 15, January 1953, p. 84.
2. *The Human Condition*, p. 127.
3. *Ibid.*, p. 133.
4. Hannah Arendt assumes throughout her works a secular world-view with no religious assurance of eternal life.
5. *The Human Condition*, p. 176.
6. *idion* in Greek.
7. *The Human Condition*, p. 165.
8. *On Revolution*, p. 63.
9. pp. 3–4.
10. *The Human Condition*, p. 24.
11. She has some interesting speculations in *On Revolution* (p. 10) as to the possible significance of the notion of a violent pre-political State of Nature.
12. p. 57.
13. *The Human Condition*, p. 234.
14. Chapter IV. She has also summed up the differences and relations between power and violence in Section II of her recent essay *On Violence*.
15. *On Revolution*, p. 148.

16. *The Human Condition*, p. 63.
17. Her essay, 'What is Freedom', reprinted in *Between Past and Future*, is mainly concerned with rebutting the accepted tradition.
18. *The Human Condition*, p. 157.
19. *On Revolution*, p. 120.
20. This is so much the case that even where a previous writer, for instance de Tocqueville, *has* talked about them, he is commonly read as if he were a Mill-type liberal, and his emphasis on the political nature of freedom is ignored.
21. *On Revolution*, pp. 271–2.
22. *Ibid.*, pp. 269–72.
23. *The Human Condition*, p. 205.

CHAPTER FOUR

1. *The Human Condition*, p. 5.
2. Printed in *Between Past and Future*.
3. The account given here draws on all Hannah Arendt's writings, but see e.g. *The Human Condition*, pp. 11, 45–53, 81–3, 119–22, 133, 138, 146–53, 187, 229–33; also *Between Past and Future*, pp. 185–96, 208–11.
4. p. 78.
5. See especially *The Human Condition*, pp. 27–44.
6. *Ibid.*, p. 45.
7. *Between Past and Future*, pp. 89–90.
8. *The Human Condition*, p. 132.
9. *Ibid.*, p. 237.
10. *On Revolution*, p. 13.
11. *Ibid.*, p. 54.
12. *Ibid.*, p. 58.
13. *The Human Condition*, p. 105.
14. *Ibid.*, p. 78.
15. *On Revolution*, p. 219.
16. *Ibid.*, Chapter VI, for Hannah Arendt's views on Parties and Councils.
17. 'Rosa Luxemburg: 1871–1919', in *Men in Dark Times*.
18. *Between Past and Future*, p. 89.
19. p. 101.
20. p. 36.
21. See e.g. *Between Past and Future*, pp. 198–200.

22. See e.g. *The Human Condition*, pp. 35–8.
23. *Ibid.*, pp. 190–6.
24. *Ibid.*, p. 115.
25. *Ibid.*, p. 194.
26. See e.g. *ibid.*, p. 294.
27. pp. 62–3.

CHAPTER FIVE

1. Reprinted in *Between Past and Future*.
2. *Ibid.*, pp. 219–23.
3. *The Human Condition*, p. 234.
4. *Between Past and Future*, p. 224.
5. See *The Methodology of the Social Sciences*, ed. Shils and Finch, 1949. For the essays on 'Politics as a Vocation' and 'Science as a Vocation' see *From Max Weber*, ed. Gerth and Mills, 1948.
6. For a description of a classic nineteenth-century example see M. Cowling: *Mill and Liberalism*.
7. 'On Humanity in Dark Times: Thoughts about Lessing', in *Men in Dark Times*.
8. *On Revolution*, p. 229.
9. In *Philosophy, Politics and Society*, 3rd Series, ed. Laslett and Runciman, 1967.
10. pp. 6–8.
11. *Between Past and Future*, p. 95.
12. As a matter of fact it is quite common for works of social science to contain both 'opinion' in Hannah Arendt's sense and 'truth' in the sense of statistics, in an uneasy combination in which the statistics do not establish the opinion, nor the opinion provide a good reason for the collection of the statistics.
13. p. 14.
14. See Bibliography for examples of works by these writers.
15. Quoted in Chapter 2 above.
16. 1962, revised edition 1964.
17. *On Revolution*, p. 274.

Select Bibliography

HANNAH ARENDT'S WORKS

Only the complete books, together with articles or collections of essays particularly relevant to the present work, are given here.

The Origins of Totalitarianism, 2nd edition, Meridian Books, 1958; new edition, Harcourt, Brace & World and George Allen and Unwin, 1966; A Harvest Book, Harcourt Brace Jovanovich, 1973.

The Human Condition, The University of Chicago Press, 1958; Doubleday Anchor Books, 1959.

Between Past and Future, Faber and Faber, 1961; The Viking Press, 1968.

On Revolution, Faber and Faber, 1963; The Viking Press, 1965; Pelican, 1973.

Eichmann in Jerusalem, The Viking Press, 1963; Faber and Faber, 1963.

Men in Dark Times, Harcourt, Brace & World, 1968; Jonathan Cape, 1970; Pelican, 1973.

On Violence, Harcourt, Brace & World, 1970; Allen Lane The Penguin Press, 1970.

Crises of the Republic, Harcourt Brace Jovanovich, 1972; Pelican, 1973.

'Truth and Politics', in *Philosophy, Politics and Society*, 3rd Series, Laslett, Peter, and Runciman, W. G., eds., Barnes and Noble, 1967.

'Peace or Armistice in the Near East', *Review of Politics*, Vol. 12, No. 1, January 1950.

'A Reply' to Eric Voegelin's review of *The Origins of Totalitarianism*, *Review of Politics*, Vol. 15, January 1953.

Select Bibliography

SOME REPRESENTATIVE WORKS OF CONTEMPORARY POLITICAL STUDY

1. *Analytical Political Philosophy:*
   Anthony Quinton (ed.), *Political Philosophy*, Oxford University Press, 1967. (A collection of articles. See especially the Introduction for a statement of the nature and purpose of political philosophy completely contrary to Hannah Arendt's views.)

2. *Political Science:*
   W. J. M. Mackenzie, *Politics and Social Science*, Penguin Books, 1967.
   David Easton, *The Political System*, Knopf, New York, 1953.
   R. A. Dahl, *Modern Political Analysis*, Prentice-Hall, 1970.
   S. M. Lipset, *Political Man*, Heinemann, 1960.
   Gabriel Almond and James Coleman, *The Politics of Developing Areas*, Princeton University Press, 1960.

3. *Reflective Political Thinking of a type comparable with Hannah Arendt's:*
   Eric Voegelin, *The New Science of Politics*, University of Chicago Press, 1952.
   Bertrand de Jouvenel, *On Power*, Viking Press, 1948; *Sovereignty*, Cambridge University Press, 1957.
   Michael Oakeshott, *Rationalism in Politics and Other Essays*, Methuen, 1962.
   Simone Weil, *Selected Essays 1934–43*, ed. Richard Rees, Oxford University Press, 1962.

OTHER WORKS REFERRED TO IN THIS BOOK

B. Crick, *In Defence of Politics*, Penguin Books, 1962.

M. Weber, *The Methodology of the Social Sciences*, ed. Shils and Finch, Free Press, 1949.

Gerth and Mills (ed.), *From Max Weber*, Routledge and Kegan Paul, 1948.

M. Cowling, *Mill and Liberalism*, Cambridge University Press, 1963.

E. H. Gombrich, *Art and Illusion*, Phaidon Press, 1960.

Index